Tri the Journey

A Woman's Inspirational Guide to Becoming a Triathlete in 12 Weeks

Libby Hurley and Betsy Noxon

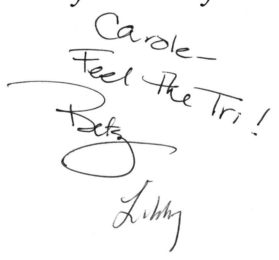

Carole—
Feel the Tri!

Betsy

Libby

Printed in the United States of America
ISBN: 978-1-935254-35-5

Cover Design by NorLightsPress Graphic Department
Book Design by Nadene Carter
Photo Credits:
    Valley Lo Club (cover photo location),
    Art Shay, cover photo,
        (individuals in photo—from left to right: Betsy Noxon,
        Joni Dobson, Libby Hurley, Hope Martin, Nancy Hurst),
    Suzann McKenna for photos throughout the book.

First printing, 2011

Dedication

Libby: To my parents Mary and Rod, who always believed in me even when I had doubts. Thank you for your selfless love, kind example, and tender guidance. Thanks to my sisters Barb and Sue, who always made me feel special. I will always look up to both of you. To my awesome husband Craig, who has been by my side for the entire journey. With your love and support I was able to follow my passion and build on my dreams. Thank you for your strength and for being the rock for our family. Thanks to God for all of my beautiful blessings.

Betsy: In memory of my dad—an inspiration to me in countless ways, who is with me in spirit on my tri journey. To my mom for her support and love. To my husband, Bruce, who always believes in me and tri's with me.

Acknowledgement

We'd like to thank each of the Together We Tri featured athletes in the book: Joni, Pam, Mervet, Alice, Julie, Nancy, Karen, Kathy, Jamie, Kim, Yvette, Eileen, Maura, and Elyse for sharing their stories. They are all strong, determined women who continue to inspire many people.

We'd also like to thank the TWT coaches who contributed their expertise to the book: Mary Bradbury, Hope Martin, and Matt Dublin. In addition, we appreciate the expertise of Deb Ognar, R.D., Jennifer Fox, PT, CSCS, and Linda Burry, M. Ed.

We'd like to acknowledge and thank Valley Lo for allowing us to shoot the cover photo at their beautiful lakefront location. A special thanks to Art Shay for taking the cover photo—it was a joy to see him at work and be part of his portfolio.

We'd also like to thank Suzanne McKenna, a triathlete herself, for shooting the athlete, swim, and gear photos. Her exceptional photographic eye and digital expertise were tireless and much appreciated.

We couldn't have completed this project without the help of our literary agent Krista Goering, our publishers at NorLightsPress, Sammie and Dee Justesen, and Nadene Carter, and our publicity manager, Jennifer Gordon.

Contents

FOREWORD

by Libby Hurley

IN MAY OF 1997, I STOOD AT THE finish line of the Escape From Alcatraz Triathlon, watching men and women of all shapes and sizes cross the line. Earlier in the day these athletes were taken by boat to Alcatraz Island to complete a one-and-a-half mile swim in 53-degree water, then a one-mile run to transition, and finally, an 18-mile hilly bike ride followed by an eight mile run. Part of their run included the notorious sand ladder—a combination of sand and about 400 uneven log steps.

As I cheered each person across the finish line, a flame inside me grew hotter by the minute. I wanted to be out there with them, raising my arms in victory, screaming with exhilaration, and rejoicing. Many of the athletes wept tears of joy, and I cried along with them.

I wiped the tears from my eyes, turned to my husband Craig, and said, "Next year I'm doing this."

He looked surprised for a moment, then hugged me and said, "Go for it, hon."

A year later, I did enter the Escape From Alcatraz Triathlon. My performance wasn't fast, nor was it pretty, but I finished the course. With that event I unleashed the inner athlete who'd been screaming at me for ten years.

Reality Sets In

Years earlier I was a fast, strong, swimmer who took to the water before I could crawl. During grade school I awakened at five o'clock each morning for a swimming workout, then returned in the afternoons for more training. I went to the state championships every year and broke several state records. Coaches told me I had Olympic potential. Although I never reached that potential, the positive experience with swimming gave me a spark that wouldn't die. Watching Escape From Alcatraz fanned that spark into a flame.

When the reality of the triathlon challenge sank in, I felt excited and terrified. Who was I to think I could become a triathlete? I hadn't swum in years. I didn't even own a bike and disliked running. Yet I couldn't stop thinking about the triathlon. What if I *could* do it?

During this time I worked as a physician's assistant in neurology, so I asked medical friends how to go about training. No one had a clue. I knew plenty of runners and swimmers, but no triathletes. To figure it all out, I collected books on triathlons, bought a bike, and started swimming, biking, and running. I had no idea what a transition meant—much less how to set one up for race day. Although I felt confident I could make it through the swim, I had no clue about strategies for climbing hills on a bike and shifting gears to save your legs for the run. I had no concept of proper running form but jumped right in and tried to figure everything out along the way. I now realize nutrition is the fourth event, but on that first race knew nothing about refueling during training or on race day. I drank water at my transition and on my bike, but nothing else. It's a wonder I didn't pass out from dehydration.

After reading several books on triathlons, I still felt intimidated and clueless. But, I persevered. As I began my training adventures, I bought a new pair of running shoes and logged every workout. Initially, I exercised four days a week, switching between running, biking, and swimming. As I began running, I literally shuffled two minutes, then walked for two minutes. Before long I was running a mile, then two, then three. I kept adding minutes each week, building up to the eight miles I needed for race day. My bike was a stranger to me at first, but after doing the same slow build, starting with a 20-minute ride, then a 30-minute, and eventually two-hour rides with hills, I began to enjoy my workouts and felt pride with each accomplishment. I was getting in shape, shedding pounds, and felt like an athlete again. I started to believe I could pull this off.

I logged countless hours of swimming, biking, and running before race day finally arrived—bringing anticipation, fear, and six trips to the porta potty. Before joining the other competitors on a boat that would drop us off in front of Alcatraz, I received the start time for my wave, had my arms and legs marked with my race number, and set up my transition. During the boat ride I stared at all the other athletes and asked myself, "What am I doing here? How did I get into this?" Everyone around me looked like super heroes. Was I ready for this?

My First Race

When the start gun began firing, athletes jumped into the icy water in waves, and my wave was getting closer. It was now or never: The moment of decision. Should I stay on the boat and wallow in fear, or take a leap of faith that I was ready and could make it to the end?

When the gun went off for my group, I jumped into the freezing bay with a rush of emotions. *Here I go! My day is here! Hello, inner athlete!* The water was shockingly cold, even in a wetsuit and a thermal cap. My heart raced as I came up for air and began swimming. I panicked through the first few strokes and gasped at the rush of flailing arms around me, but then found my stroke—the familiar rhythm that brought me blue ribbons and gold medals in high school. Midway through the race I turned on my back, stared at the sky, and thanked God for this journey. I gave the heavens a big smile and laughed out loud. I was on my way to becoming a triathlete, achieving the first athletic goal I'd set for myself in decades. Right then, in the middle of the bay, I knew I'd never feel the same about any challenges I might face during my life. I had taken a leap of faith and was lucky enough to be part of something remarkable.

The Race: My Personal Victory

I finished the swim and ran with pure joy to my first race transition. And although I lost my bike in the crowd and finding it took much longer than expected, nothing fazed me. I was doing this. The weather was a perfect 68 degrees and sunlight peeked through the clouds. I took my time and enjoyed the strength of all the athletes around me, wishing them all good luck. I remained in awe as practically everyone passed me. Some of the hills were more than challenging, but I kept going until after 18 miles, when I made it back for my final leg of the race. All along I saw smiling faces encouraging me to do my best, dig deep, and keep up the good work. The run was difficult, and as we headed out, I couldn't help noticing other athletes sprinting to their finish. I could hardly wait to be there.

By the time I reached the famous sand steps on Baker Beach, they felt more like a sand slide. I took a moment to look at the Golden Gate Bridge, wondering if I would always view the bay differently, knowing I'd swum in that water, biked along the border, and run on the beach. The final two miles were filled with gratitude, tears, and prayers. I sprinted the last 100 yards as the announcer called my race number and MY name. Spectators gave me high fives and cheered for me when I neared the end of the race. The delight and awe on their faces reminded me of my own emotions a year earlier.

Now it was my turn. I finished in the rear of the pack, probably one of the last to cross the line, but I made it. I searched for Craig among the crowd and flung myself into his arms, sobbing with joy. At that moment I felt my chemistry change. I, Libby Hurley, was a triathlete who'd overcome much and accomplished even more. I was empowered, transformed, and beyond grateful that God gave me this opportunity to shift my life in a new direction.

In the days following this personal victory, I wanted everyone around me to feel the joy I'd experienced. I couldn't keep this amazing accomplishment to myself. I had to let other people—especially women—know they could do this. Triathlons aren't for super-human athletes; they're designed for regular folks who want to feel healthy, strong, and accomplished. I needed to take the fear out of this venture and make it more do-able. I wanted to help others change their lives through the journey of triathlons. I developed a passion to tell anyone and everyone: "If I can do it, so can you!"

Together We Tri Is Born

Together we Tri (TWT) was born after Craig and I moved to Chicago in 2000. During our first year we trained 16 athletes, many of whom became our close friends. This journey changed all our lives. Now, after 10 seasons of training athletes with the best coaches around, we've touched the lives of over 6,000 people and watched amazing transformations.

Our athletes and their stories continually inspire me. We help them put it all together, train smart, and cross the finish line. We have athletes who win their age group and athletes with arthritis who become stronger by doing full body, tri-focused training. We have moms, daughters, and grandmas. We have people just like you—folks with a goal to feel better and try something they never imagined they could accomplish.

After 13 years of racing, I'm still celebrating the gift of triathlons. I am continually delighted to have my family cheer for me and all our athletes at each race. I feel privileged to be part of so many transformations. Craig has been my biggest supporter and watched me evolve into the confident mother of three amazing children and a competitor in three Ironman races. In my younger days, the thought of completing a 2.4-mile swim and a 112-mile bike ride, followed by a marathon of 26.2 miles seemed completely out of reach. Now this accomplishment belongs to me—and it's mine for the rest of my life.

On race days, my husband, children, parents, and sisters hold signs that say, "Libby, you are my Ironman." Now I know how to train with the best of them. I know a little about belief and a lot about desire: you can do anything you put your mind to.

Life is truly remarkable. I feel so blessed I was on the sidelines in 1997, where I received the nudge to *TRI the Journey*. I hope this book will inspire you to do the same.

INTRODUCTION

TAKE A DEEP BREATH and jump into the world of triathlon.

When you make the leap, be prepared to transform your life beyond all expectations. As you follow in the footsteps of women before you and embrace the Together We Tri program, you'll become a stronger swimmer, cyclist, runner—and more. You'll embark on a dynamic, fulfilling journey; a journey thousands of women are discovering and telling others about: the journey of becoming a triathlete.

Perhaps you've admired triathletes, wondering who they are and how they become race ready. In this book you'll find stories from women who decided to accept this challenge. Most joined Together We Tri to prepare for a triathlon the right way, experience it with others, and have fun. You'll share their fears and accomplishments in stories that are funny, touching, and sometimes serious. From these stories you'll learn what worked and what didn't work in training and races. You'll realize you aren't alone with your questions and concerns. Before you start training, be sure you get clearance from your physician to begin a regimented exercise program.

You'll love the unique Together We Tri 12-week program that helps you adapt training to a busy life. We provide information about triathlons, answer your burning questions, and help you train for your own events. We've included photos, insider coaching tips, and firsthand accounts from experts and first timers. We encourage you to use the TRI Note pages at the end of the book to record your thoughts, inspiration, struggles, and accomplishments, plus things you want to share with your family and friends.

Your inner athlete is calling you—yearning for a challenge and aching to fulfill your dreams. Your life will transform during this journey, and at the end you'll achieve the unthinkable—gaining strength, confidence, memories, and friends, and a new identity of becoming a triathlete. Onward!

SECTION I

You Can Tri

NOTES

CHAPTER 1

Begin the Journey

"People may doubt what you say,
but they will believe what you do."
—Lewis Cass

FOR MANY WOMEN, COMPLETING a triathlon transcends all expectations. Your life is transformed and forever altered. Confidence soars and you feel as though you can accomplish anything. As Joni explains below, this new *can do* attitude will help you deal with all kinds of challenges. Brace yourself for a life-changing experience!

Joni Dobson

Doing a triathlon was something that never entered Joni Dobson's mind. She didn't consider herself an athlete, although she was active in recreational sports as a young girl—dabbling in golf, tennis, skiing, and swimming. She prided herself on long distance lap swimming—setting a goal at the age of 10 to swim a mile and doing it. As Joni became a teenager, her father (an avid golfer) took her to the driving range to practice several times a week. On one of her backswings, she pivoted her knee too far and it collapsed, swelling immediately. Their physician confirmed she'd chipped a bone near her knee cap. Since then, Joni shied away from rigorous activities and was frightened to take up running, anxious about hurting her knee.

As time went on and she became busy with work and family, recreational sports fell to the wayside. Unfortunately, by the time her life finally settled down, she'd developed severe degenerative arthritis in both knees, because of her past golf injury. To stay active and ease the knee pain, she began swimming again for exercise.

At one of her book club meetings, a woman shared her fun experiences doing triathlons. At the age of 60, Joni's interest resurfaced again. The following week Libby spoke about triathlons to a Zumba dance class Joni attended. That was it. Joni took on the challenge and faced her deepest fears.

For 21 years Joni had feared dying young, because her mother succumbed to cancer at the age of 59. Joni worried about being healthy in her 50s and wondered if she'd live past 59. Besides the fear of cancer, to complete a triathlon she'd have to overcome her fear of cycling and open water swims, and running or walking in pain.

Joni saw her knee specialist for clearance into the program. He told her cycling was good for the knees, because it builds strength in the quadriceps. She could walk during the run to avoid pain. He added, "You know you won't win." His words didn't stop her from trying. Joni began training for a sprint triathlon, following the TWT plan. At the first group meeting she realized she wasn't the only one struggling with fears. Other women were also taking risks.

Morning workouts became a way of starting each day. She signed up for swim lessons to learn proper technique and "awaken" her inner swimmer. Despite her swim background, Joni was still afraid of open water. She worried about panicking with all the people around her, or having people swim on top of her. As she practiced open water swims and swim start simulations in the pool, she focused on keeping her composure by thinking of all the people who were supporting this journey. Her manager at IBM does triathlons and many of her co-workers helped her along the way.

Keeping balanced and in control on her new hybrid bike (more upright, with straight handlebars and wider tires than a road bike) and riding in a group also made Joni nervous. Initially, she rode in remote areas and on back streets at 5 a.m. before venturing further afield and crossing streets. She gradually built her endurance week by week in each sport until she was race ready. Joni's approach to triathlons: enjoy each sport while you're doing it. Be in the moment.

Joni's First Race

The night before the Danskin Triathlon in Pleasant Prairie, Wisconsin, Joni's son David asked her what she thought Mimi, her deceased mother, would say about racing. Joni was taken aback by the question, not knowing what her mother would have thought. She went on to race the next day, not really knowing what to expect. Despite jangled nerves at the beginning, she enjoyed each leg of her first race. She was surprised by all the positive energy at the Danskin Tri. As she rode her bike uphill against the wind, a young woman rode by her and called out, "You're doing a great job—keep going!" As she passed, Joni read a sign pinned to the other woman's back saying "Mimi, Cancer Survivor." She felt that her mom, Mimi, was right there with her cheering her on, proud that she'd taken the challenge.

Joni's children were there with her on the journey, supporting her until the end. David (who took up swimming after Joni started) encouraged her to "keep her head in the game," and her daughter, Jaime, who walks, cycles and practices yoga, decorated plates for Joni's supporters, thanking her

Joni Dobson

"balcony people." Both children and her daughter-in-law, Tasha, were at the finish line. Her willingness to step out of her comfort zone and challenge herself has continued to inspire all of her supporters to do the same.

Joni:

" I once had a passing thought that it would be amazing to enter a triathlon. Yes, me, Ms. Haven't-been-athletic-my-whole-life. Then I met Libby, who explained how I could actually do it. My initial idea was to begin the training with no big expectations and see how things went. Two triathlons later, I'm proud of what I've accomplished. The bike was the biggest obstacle for me, because I was terrified of falling. Now, although I'm still a bit leery when I start and while turning corners, I'm proud that I averaged 16 mph in the last tri and accomplished something I was certain I could never do. But, as I learned—it isn't as much about the destination as the journey.

And now here I am, one year before turning sixty, and I've finished two triathlons. The bittersweet irony is, I won FIRST PLACE in my age group in the Glenview Park Center Tri because no other 54- to 59-year-old women entered the event. I'm trying to convince every woman my age this is something you can do if you have an inkling of desire. The medal we received after finishing the Danskin Tri says: "The woman who started this race is not the same woman who finished it." Completing a tri to achieve the best times, or just to say I've done it, aren't important. My twist on being an athlete is the incorporation of the three disciplines into my lifestyle. I've learned to do my own "personal sprints" by swimming a half mile in our local pool, taking in nature on my 12-mile bike ride to our local Botanical Gardens, and walking three miles to our closest Starbucks while listening to my iPod. I feel I am winning my own wonderful, continuous race! "

Become an Athlete: Try the Distance

Triathlons are versatile and appealing to people because you can choose from several race options: the Super Sprint, Sprint, Olympic, Half Ironman, and Ironman races. These all include swim, bike, and run segments. You may choose to start with a shorter race and progress to longer races, or stick with a distance you find challenging enough. Check out the races in your area, including distances and dates, so you have plenty of time to train and prepare. Most of this information you can find online. Chances are you'll find a race that's perfect for you.

TRI Race Distances

- Sprint distance—½ mile swim, 12 mile bike, 5 K (3.1mile) run.
- Olympic distance –1.5 K (.93 mile) swim, 40 K (24.8 mile) bike, 10 K (6.2 mile) run.
- 70.3 (or Half Ironman)—1.2 mile swim, 56 mile bike, 13.1 mile run.
- Ironman—2.4 mile swim, 112 mile bike, 26.2 mile run.

We'll show you how to train for the fun, yet challenging, Sprint and Olympic races in only 12 weeks. If Joni and thousands of others can do this, so can you!

You may choose to begin with races even shorter than the standard Sprint distance. Joni's first event was a local triathlon that called for a 300-yard pool swim, a 10-mile bike ride through neighborhoods, and a 5 K run around a lake. The Super Sprint distance is gaining popularity and typically includes a 375 meter (0.25 mile) swim, a 10 K (6.2 mile) bike ride, and a 2.5 K (1.55 mile) run. Many athletes use a Super Sprint as practice while training for a longer event. This is a great event to gain confidence for your main "A" race.

Either way, the distances are short enough so you can push yourself and sprint the entire distance, but you don't have to. The race is yours to accomplish, fast or slow, regardless of your goal. With proper training, a beginner can complete a sprint distance triathlon in less than two hours. Entertainer Jennifer Lopez completed her first triathlon in Malibu at the two hour mark, only one month after giving birth to twins.

The Olympic distance is double the Sprint. Typically the swim is just under a mile, then a 24.8-mile bike ride, and a 10 K (6.2 mile) run. As you might expect, training for the Olympic race requires twice the time and distance as the Sprint distance. Some people sign up for a Sprint race during the summer before an Olympic race, then continue training by adding mileage to their base schedule. You might consider an Olympic distance race once you feel comfortable completing one or two Sprint races. Or you may enjoy the Sprint distance and participate at that level year after year. The important first step is to choose your race and set your first race goal.

For first timers, the final race time on the clock isn't the biggest marker of accomplishment. It's realizing how far you can go with a little knowledge and a safe plan. You'll soon understand that

Libby Hurley's first goal and beyond

66 My real goal when I signed up for the first triathlon was to follow through with a plan and feel good about myself. Too often in the past I'd set my sights on a goal and give up without reaching it, thanks to fear, lack of commitment, not enough time, or poor planning. After a few years of that behavior, I started feeling like a quitter. I didn't enjoy having that title dance around in my brain.

The thought of doing a triathlon created butterflies of excitement in my stomach. I decided to follow through for once—to train properly and cross the finish line, no matter what. I wanted to feel the pride of finishing something. I also yearned to be healthier and lose weight (which automatically happened completing a triathlon is mostly about the journey before the race and how 12 weeks of training can change your life.

As you note your training goals, keep them realistic and attainable. Also explore the intrinsic goals, dreaming of what else you hope to achieve on this journey to the finish line and beyond. Your goals may change over time, but begin by exploring those that will give you hope, excitement, and make you feel alive.

Goal Sheet

1. Write your goals for training or completing a race. These might include...

- finishing a race,
- achieving a specific time,
- improved fitness,
- losing weight, and
- improving in a specific sport.

as I added to my workouts). Mostly I wanted to believe I could do whatever I put my mind to. And my plan worked. Today I've completed over 50 races, helped motivate thousands of athletes, and after having three beautiful children I still carve out time to give myself the gift of health and accomplish whatever I put my mind to.

Some days are harder than others. You have to dig deep into your soul and remember how you'll be rewarded if you follow through with your plan. On those tough days, you must talk to yourself and convince your mind not to give up. But each little step toward your goal adds strength and confidence in yourself. and helps you continue. 99

2. Now think of internal goals for self-fulfillment. These might include...
   - the feeling of success when I cross the finish line,
   - setting a goal and following through,
   - proving my strength,
   - feeling healthy, proud, and powerful, and
   - being an inspiration to others.

3. List your strengths and weaknesses as an athlete.

4. What mental, physical, and emotional obstacles prevent you from sticking to a training plan?

5. What do you hope to gain from your training experience and journey?

Overcoming Obstacles: No Excuses!

We all have strengths, weaknesses, and busy lives. Each of us can think of a million excuses not to take on something that will challenge us to grow. It's easier to dismiss a challenge rather than take it head on, but think in the long run of how you will grow and what you will accomplish. Consider the big picture and all the benefits of training and doing a triathlon. These will trump your excuses. On days when you want to throw in the towel, journal about you're feelings. Some days you actually might need a break, but if it's just fear talking, make a pact with yourself that you'll try exercising for ten minutes. If you still feel negative after ten minutes, give yourself a break. However, chances are good you'll finish the workout once you start. Try to think through each of your obstacles, and then shift your thinking to "no excuses."

If you have difficulty scheduling time for yourself, you may need to think creatively. Rise before the kids two mornings a week, garner support from your spouse or significant other, or perhaps hire a babysitter one night a week to make time for workouts. Consider all the options. Examine your weekly and monthly schedule, develop an awareness of how you spend your time, and then PLAN. Map out every workout, including the hour and day, and you'll make training part of your life. After a couple of weeks, you'll get into a rhythm and feel as though you've developed a new healthy habit, while slowly sidelining unhealthy habits, such as poor eating and unhealthy behaviors. Once you assign a specific day and time to your workouts you'll begin to look forward to your Tuesday swims, your Thursday runs, or those early morning bike rides.

As you plan your schedule, find blocks of time during the day when you can make an appointment at the track, the pool, or with your bike. Let your family know training will soon become part of your weekly schedule and you'd appreciate support and understanding. Invite them to join you for workouts; a run once a week, a long cycle on the weekend, or a few laps in the pool on a warm summer day. Even your school-aged kids can ride their bikes while you run, or they can race you while you do sprint work. They can keep you company and motivated during phases of your training. A lot of bonding happens over a sweaty swim, bike ride, and run.

Invite a friend to join the journey

Consider recruiting a friend or two who will go through the journey with you, so you can pick one another up on down days and keep each other accountable. Find running clubs in your town, cycle with a group organized through a local bike shop, or join a swim team where you can talk about your triathlon so you feel more accountable for your goal. When you tell people you're training for a triathlon race at the end of the month, you'll gain support and bolster your confidence. Just verbalizing your plan makes it more real. Once you sign up for a race, you may also find support groups with the sponsor or online, including...

www.trithejourney.com

Log on and train with a virtual buddy or ask a coach for tips.

Use your training journal to keep track of daily workouts, your accomplishments, and your thoughts about the challenges. Soon you'll look back and view your progress in black and white, showing how much stronger you're getting. The prompts listed in the back of this book will help you get started. We encourage you to be creative—even draw pictures if you want—and adapt the space so it works for you. You'll refer back to your TRI Notes from time to time and be amazed at how far you've come.

Reviewing your goals and accomplishments helps keep you motivated to continue working hard. How do you want to feel and look as you cross the finish line? Who will you inspire by achieving this goal? Answering these questions and defining your goals will give you the opportunity to look back and say, "Oh, yeah, that's why I started this journey."

Feel free to take notes on the side of the pages, at the end of some chapters, or in the back of the book in the TRI Notes section if you want to log your workouts. You need to be aware of changes in your body and your attitude. Journaling will help you gain confidence in your abilities. No matter what hurdles you face, with a little positive thinking and a no-excuses attitude, you can make this work. As you begin seeing the rewards, you'll feel stronger mentally and physically—and nothing will stand in your way.

Progress checks will keep you going

Check in with your goals from time to time and reset them as you continue training. When you reach a goal and see results, you'll be ready for the next phase of the program. Bump the intensity, plan a longer training session, or do a brick workout. If you're having a tough week, set mini-goals to get you through. Don't let one discouraging workout get you down. Jump right back in and look back on what you've accomplished instead of what you missed.

If one of your goals is to get fit and lose weight, before starting this program note your starting weight and take measurements of your arms, hips, and waist for your journal. Consider trying to lose a few pounds before you start the training program, as your appetite will increase as your training progresses. If you are wanting to optimize weight loss make sure you are aware of how much you are eating and make good food choices. Re-take these readings after four, eight, and twelve weeks to help track your progress and see how you're doing with the goals you set. Don't hesitate to make adjustments as needed. Be realistic so you don't set yourself up for disappointments.

COACH TIP

"Set goals, go back to review them, and revise as needed. Don't get discouraged."

-Hope Martin
Together We Tri Trainer

Key Points

1. Set reasonable goals for yourself.
2. Take baby steps toward your goal. Don't let yourself feel overwhelmed by your final race distance.
3. No excuses!
4. Planning ahead will help you overcome obstacles.
5. Find a friend who'll train with you, such as a *Tri the Journey* buddy - www.trithejourney.com.
6. Periodic progress checks will help you stay motivated.
7. Think positive!

NOTES

CHAPTER 2

Build Your Tri Locker

Great change may not happen right away, but with effort,
even the difficult may become easy.
— Bill Blackman

WHEN PAM TIERNEY STARTED the 12-week triathlon train-
ing program, she'd never done anything just for herself. As the oldest
of five children in a family that focused on group activities such as
swimming, tennis, or golf, Pam participated in these sports with her
siblings for the sake of convenience. In school, fitting in with her
peers was important, so she tended to do what they wanted to do.
Once she entered the working world in media sales, she often found
herself bending to the needs of supervisors and clients.

Pam Tierney

"Everything in my life seemed outwardly focused, toward others. I
used to joke that no one ever asked how I was doing," Pam explained.
She never anticipated that finding the sport of triathlon would finally
enable her to do something for herself and change her focus.

For her birthday that year, Pam gave herself personal training
sessions. One day while working out, her trainer told her about the

tri program Libby was organizing. With her trainer's support, Pam signed up for TWT. To begin training, she needed a bike. She didn't spend much for the bicycle, but did invest in a good pair of bike shorts so she could cycle in comfort. To save money she rented a wetsuit and wore running shoes she already owned. As she continued doing more events over three years, Pam built up her tri locker by adding bike shoes, clips, and a new, padded tri bathing suit.

Pam Begins Training

During the 12-week training, Pam continued assessing her fitness as she gained both strength and endurance. Although she hadn't been on a swim team in years and had never swum without a line below her, she practiced swim drills—spotting and learning to breathe on both sides of her body while doing the freestyle. While swimming in the lake, she learned to sight by looking up every fourth stroke at a building or tree to help navigate. That way she wouldn't veer off course when swimming in the lake. Pam also learned about the transition area (more on this in Chapter 9) and the need to practice at least a dozen times so she wasn't fumbling for her gear. By following the weekly schedule and listening to her coach's tips, she felt confident with the program. Pam especially related to the nutrition and hydration tips, like drinking water and/or electrolytes every 15 minutes or so on the bike, and eating a gel when working out for over an hour. Libby's coaches and program prepared her for almost any scenario on the course. Running was her most challenging sport of the tri, but she kept working until she was able to run more than she walked. She kept setting distance goals for herself, such as run to that tree, run to that sign, sprint to that bench.

Pam's First Race

The program took all the mystery out of doing a triathlon, giving her the tools to be successful. Pam gained confidence along her journey, and by the day of the Danskin race when she awakened at five in the morning for the one-hour drive to Wisconsin, she felt fully prepared for the events ahead. She cried with happiness during the bus ride from the parking lot to the starting line. She felt amazed at her journey and overjoyed because she was doing this for herself.

As she waded into the lake to start the race with other women in her wave, the woman beside her said, "You must've done this before. You're so calm!"

"No, this is my first race," Pam said, "but I feel ready." She had trained for this moment and it belonged to her.

As Pam worked her way around the course, she told herself she'd be happy to finish. After all, her goal that morning was to just show up. While running the 3.1 miles, she figured her time and realized if she ran a little faster, she'd finish in under two hours. So she picked up her pace, going back to her habit of finding a target ahead of her and running to it. When she dropped back to a walk, she made it a brisker walk than before. She breathed hard and pumped her arms, concentrating until the end. She crossed the line in one hour and 58 minutes, feeling like a new woman.

Completing her first triathlon was a pivotal moment in Pam's life. Her soaring confidence gave her the courage to take another leap and change careers, from working in advertising sales to becoming an actress and voiceover professional, a new passion for her.

Pam completed four more triathlons the following year and became a mentor to other women starting their tri journey.

Pam Tierney

Pam:

66 The woman I was when I started this tri program is far from the woman I am today. This was a pivotal point, and some days I'm astonished at where this journey has taken me. 99

Goggles to Running Shoes: A No-nonsense Guide to Tri Equipment

Wet hair, bug-eyed goggles, sticky-sweaty shirts, and unsightly padded bike shorts are all part of athletics. You'll enjoy finding your tri gear and feeling like a real athlete. This isn't the time to worry about how you look—we all have not-so-flattering parts of our bodies. Lord knows, most of us are not comfortable with our bum flying in the wind for all to see. Just know everyone faces body image insecurities, but other people don't have time to judge you, because we're all focusing on our own performances. No one feels perfect. Try to let go. Cover up what you want to cover up, focus on your training, and ignore the little voice that whispers about your imperfections. The more you feel the part, the more you will train, and the better prepared you'll be.

Joni is the first to agree with this advice. While she was running in a triathlon, someone running past her shouted, "Hey, did you know your pants are on backwards?" Joni, being concerned about how she looked, stopped, took off her shorts, and turned them around. Now, realizing this added time to her race, Joni advises others not to worry about how you look—just get out there and do it.

Your first thought, like ours, might be: "Three sports, lots of stuff!" But this needn't be the case, because you can get by with basic equipment you may already own. In fact, less is better, because transition times add to your total time on race day. Minimal equipment will give you faster transitions from sport to sport. You can begin training with the following items:

- swimsuit and tri suit (wetsuit - optional), goggles, swim cap,
- bike and helmet (maybe bike shoes that clip onto your pedals),
- running shoes (socks, shorts, running bra for us ladies).

Get comfortable wearing your gear

You may feel odd at first, especially if you aren't happy with your body size and shape. Although we understand this may be difficult, try to love your body as it is. Your body is remarkable, and during this training you'll often be in a swim suit, or tri suit, at the pool or a lake. Forget about how you look and concentrate on becoming stronger, leaner, and faster. Jump into the pool and get moving! We never swim without a swim cap or goggles. Hair in the face while swimming is distracting. Goggles keep your eyes safe from chlorine or debris in the water, help you swim straight, and prevent sun glare; a practical item for race day comfort.

We were thankful to have tinted goggles on the morning of the Danskin race in June. The sun was directly across from the starting point in the lake and right in our faces. The goggles helped us stay on course.

Using a wetsuit for the swim is a good option if you can rent or buy one. A wetsuit will keep you warm on early morning lake swims, cut your swim time anywhere from two to four minutes, reserve your energy for the bike and run, and give you extra buoyancy and good positioning.

If possible, try on different types and sizes of wetsuits. A sleeveless suit is less restrictive, while a suit with sleeves gives more buoyancy and speed. Either way, the suit will keep you warm in cold water. Keep in mind that if the water temperature is above 82 degrees Fahrenheit, race directors won't let competitors wear a wetsuit. You can choose to wear your suit for comfort, but you won't qualify for age group awards because the suit gives you an advantage over those not suited up.

Betsy's first wetsuit swim

Libby contacted Zoot, a wetsuit manufacturer, to bring a variety of suits poolside so our TWT group could try them while swimming laps in the pool. At the pool's edge, we each tried on a suit after spraying ourselves with Suit Juice, a lubricant to help to ease on the tight fitting, thick, neoprene garments. I sprayed the juice liberally on my arms and legs and neck, excited to try this new thing and see how it felt—both dry and wet. Our guides advised us not to dig our nails into the suit as we pulled it up and on, as this would damage the material. We all slowly eased into our new skin.

As I glanced at the others and then at myself, I realized we all looked like shiny black whales—sleek and ready to swim. In the suits, we'd be warm and fast. Some women think the tight suits make them look heavier, but I felt that slipping into a wetsuit at the poolside with the group of other women was non-threatening and a good opportunity to try something new. I was sold on wetsuits the moment I jumped into the pool and took my first stroke, gliding smoothly through the water. I popped up effortlessly from the water—my whole body, hips and all, was suddenly buoyant. With each stroke the water skimmed over me. When I took a stroke, my suited arm reminded me of a dolphin's skin. Before I knew it, I reached the wall—the end of the 25-yard length of the pool. I was swimming faster than I ever had before. Wetsuits cost between one and three hundred dollars, so take your time shopping and seek expert advice about what's right for you. If you decide to invest in a suit, keep in mind that your body may change from year to year.

Wetsuit/swim equipment

Libby's two wetsuits

Over the years I've purchased a couple of wetsuits to accommodate my fluctuating weight. My first suit was before having babies; I purchased the next suit after my first child was born. After my second child, when time for the next race rolled around I pulled out my suit and brought it to the race. Though I hadn't trained in the suit for months, I brought it along not only for warmth and buoyancy, but also to cover my post-baby body. Let's be real here—who wants to flaunt their body shortly after delivery? Not me.

So I sprayed the suit liberally with Pam cooking spray (olive essence flavor) and began squeezing into my wetsuit to make myself into a nice taught package: race ready. Unfortunately, the squeeze was worse than I had envisioned. Instead of a pulled together, supported athlete, I felt more like a sausage. I tugged, pulled, and gyrated. After about 30 minutes and the help of five fellow Triangels, I got into my wetsuit and zipped it.

Despite my good intentions, the swim was miserable because of the tight suit. I felt like I couldn't take a full breath. Talk about motivation! For my next race, would I purchase a third wetsuit, or would I get in shape and lose weight? I learned two things: make sure your suit fits before the race, and if you work hard enough, you CAN get back into the wetsuit you already own—eventually.

Your bike: get ready to ride

After the swim, you'll emerge from the water and mount your bike for the cycle portion of the race. For this, you'll need a bike and a helmet. Your local bike shop can advise you on options and get you fitted. If you need to purchase a new bike, this will be your biggest expense. Bikes come with one of two types of pedals: a flat pedal to fit your running shoe, or clip pedals that fit special cycling shoes fitted to the pedal. With the clip pedal, you are clipped into your bike, therefore, your foot is secure as it rotates or spins around, giving you maximum pull and push. As a result, your pedal stroke will be more even, stronger, and faster than if you aren't clipped in.

Many first time "clippers" are intimidated about being "stuck" to their bikes, but after practicing this becomes second nature. We suggest you practice on a baseball field or grassy area for safety until you feel comfortable clipping in and out on the road. If you have access to a stationary trainer, you can secure your bike in the trainer (available for purchase at bike, sporting good stores, or online) and practice pedaling, stopping, and clipping in and out without falling. Even the best of us occasionally forget to clip out and do the tilt over. If you are falling down, aim for the grass. As with anything else, practice makes perfect.

Cannondale Road Bike

If you already own a bike, you may need to have it tuned up, or shop for a new one that will safely carry you 12 or 24 miles. An expert at the bike shop should check the following:

- bike brake wires, break calipers (mechanism that works the breaks), and pads to be sure they're working appropriately and not rubbing on the wheels,
- wheels and spokes are straight and don't wobble,
- derailer/gear alignment and settings so you can adequately shift gears,
- seat and seat post are properly centered and tightened,
- headset and handlebars are aligned and tightened correctly,

- chain is not overstretched and in need of replacement (It's typically replaced at 2,000 miles),
- spin wheels to check if bearings are broken or grinding,
- spin cranks (pedals) to check for tightness.

You can train on whatever bike you have for the first year of racing. As long as the bike fits you, you can continue racing on it as long as you wish. If you need or want a new bike, make sure you go to a bike shop and get fitted for size — the most important aspect of your bike purchase. For example, if you know you fit on a 54-inch frame, you can then shop around for the right price or even find a used bike on Craig's List. Mountain bikes are common in the women's races, but feel free to use a hybrid, a tri bike, or a road bike that fits your price range.

Once you decide which bike to use for your training and race, have a local bike shop help you make the bike ready for training and race day. Joni bought a hybrid bike (a mix between a road and mountain bike), because its straight handle bars allowed her to sit more upright, compared to a road bike with handle bars curved under, which is more aerodynamic, but creates a need for you to stretch forward. Joni felt more stable on a little thicker tire than the thin tire of the road bike, and the hybrid was versatile enough for racing or comfortably riding to the store and back.

Your best protection, a good helmet

A helmet is your best protection on the road as you cycle. Helmets are no longer geeky; they're the norm — a must-have. You can't ride in a race without a helmet. All new helmets have to pass a safety requirement, so if you own a cheap helmet that's a few years old, you should upgrade. When you purchase a helmet, look for an adjustable model so you can mold the fit to your head. For a good fit, adjust the chin strap so there's room to place two fingers in between the strap and your chin without discomfort. More than two fingers and it's too loose. The actual helmet should rest on your forehead. If it's above your forehead, you aren't getting adequate protection. The helmet should be close to the same circumference of your head. When you place the helmet on your head and have your straps properly adjusted, the helmet shouldn't move when you shake or nod your head. If you feel the helmet sliding, you need to adjust the fit or get a smaller size. If you have doubts about your helmet, visit a bike shop and have them properly fit you. This is a vital safety measure, so please don't take chances by wearing a poorly fitted helmet.

Don't cycle without your helmet. One of our athletes drove over an hour on race morning and by mistake left her helmet at home. Over the loud speaker, the announcer asked if anyone had an extra helmet for a fellow athlete. After several minutes someone came forward with a spare. But don't tempt fate by leaving home without yours. After months of diligent training, you deserve your reward.

Padded cycling shorts

Since you'll be riding long distances while training (sometimes over an hour), it's a good idea to buy a pair of padded cycling shorts. They are fitted tight around your legs to keep the wind out (and bugs and bees from flying in) and will keep you comfortable while you're seated for long rides. The tight fit is also referred to as a compression short, which helps with circulation and muscle recovery. Tri shorts have less padding to make it easier to run following the cycling portion of the race. For brick training, tri shorts (great to race in) have just enough padding to make you comfortable for the whole race, from swim to short to medium length rides followed by short to medium length runs.

Biking gloves

Biking gloves will help protect your palms on bumpy rides. Rider's palsy is a condition whereby the ulnar nerve becomes irritated from compression or positioning, jarring rides, and gripping the handlebars too tight. If you experience numbness while riding, gloves will definitely help alleviate that issue. Gloves also keep your hands warm during long rides on cool days. Remember not to grip your handlebars too tight, causing strain on your wrists, arms, and upper body.

The saddle

You have several choices for a bike seat, (or saddle). Some are ultra-padded, while others are sleek and aerodynamic—but not all that comfortable at first. Typically, as you train, your posterior grows accustomed to the saddle and you don't notice the discomfort. Still, comfort is key, so if your seat bothers you, trade it for a padded seat. New devices can measure the width of your sits bones to determine which seat is best for you. Many cycle shops offer this service.

~~~~

When you've completed the cycling leg of the race, you'll be switching your clippers for running shoes. Running shoes, socks, shorts, and a light weight shirt are essential items for the run, (some folks will prefer a tri suit instead of socks, shorts, or top) even if you choose to walk. You might be surprised to know that many people walk the on-foot portion of the race. So, if you know you aren't a runner and don't aspire to ever be one, don't let that hold you back. You can join the group of walkers and still complete the race.

Joni has arthritis in her knees and no cartilage, so running was impossible, but that didn't stop her from training and racing. If you have physical problems, be sure to consult your physician before you begin training, but don't let a negative attitude or the fact that you're a walker get in your way. You can do it!

Running shoes

A good pair of running shoes makes all the difference in the world. Running shoes provide cushioning, stability, and protection to your feet while you put in the miles.

Top brand, high tech running shoes can cost well over $100, but you don't have to go this route for good quality shoes, especially since you'll need to replace them periodically. Running shoes should be replaced every 300 to 500 hundred miles, because they wear down with use. Depending on your gait or how your foot strikes the ground, you might need a cushioned shoe versus a stability shoe. You may have heard about pronation, or how the foot rolls when it strikes the ground. People either pronate, under pronate, or have normal pronation. With over pronating, when you run or walk the foot first touches the ground on the inside and you push off your big toe to propel forward. In this case, your ankle rolls slightly inward. Under pronation means your foot strikes on the outside. A normal pronator's foot strikes fairly flat, not rolling significantly to either side. Whatever your gait, the proper shoe will help prevent injuries

If you don't know what type of shoe is best for you, visit a professional running store where they can analyze your run and help fit you with the proper footwear. Bring an old pair of shoes to the store so they can see the wear patterns on the bottom. They will be able to tell how you pronate by checking where your shoe is worn out. Since you'll be running or walking many miles in preparation for the race, wearing a comfortable shoe that works for your foot and gait goes a long way.

Compared to cycling socks, running socks are thicker and provide more cushion for long, weight-bearing runs.

Sunblock essentials

A good pair of lightweight sunglasses is essential to keep the sun and bugs out of your eyes. We also recommend a breathable hat to keep the sun off your head. Don't forget to apply sunscreen—even on a cloudy day

If you're concerned about equipment malfunction, don't worry. By race day, if you follow our plan, you'll have practiced all areas of the tri, and you'll know how to recover in any situation.

We advise you to move slowly with equipment purchases, building on what you already own. Ask for recommendations from friends, family, trainers, and other athletes. You can learn from their mistakes.

Have fun building your tri locker! And remember, if you look the part, before long you'll start *feeling* the part and be well on your way to becoming a triathlete and transforming into something you never thought possible. Triathlon, here you come!

Key Points

Gradually build your tri locker. Necessary items include...

- swimsuit, tri suit, and wetsuit (optional), goggles, swim cap,
- bicycle suitable for at least a 12 mile trip,
- bike helmet,
- optional, cycling shoes that clip onto your pedals,
- biking gloves,
- running shoes,
- socks, shorts, and a running bra,
- sunglasses and hat,
- Sprint Tri distance: 1/2 mile swim, 12 mile bike, 3.1 mile run (5K),
- Olympic Tri distance: 1.5 K (.93 mile) swim, 40 K (24.8 mile) bike, 10 K (6.2 mile) run.

NOTES

CHAPTER 3

Sharpen Your Skills

*"People become quite remarkable when they start thinking
they can do things. When they believe in themselves,
they have the first secret of success."*
—Norman Vincent Peale

BORN AND RAISED IN JORDAN in the Middle East, Mervet
Ghbari never learned to ride a bike or swim, because her culture
considered straddling a bike or showing skin inappropriate. After
moving to the United States in her mid-20s, she discovered exercise
was a great way to get fit.

Mervet Ghbari

At age 30, Mervet was shopping for camping gear with her
boyfriend when they saw a bike on sale for $75. On a whim and out
of curiosity, she bought it and her boyfriend taught her how to ride.
This was something fun for them to do together. As for running, she
learned about technique and training from reading a book. From this
point, her life was changed forever.

"I first started running two to three miles. When a co-worker told me she ran five miles, it seemed unbelievable she could run that long. When I finally worked up to five miles, it felt incredible," says Mervet. Running led her to compete in a half-marathon, but she feared long term endurance running would be too hard on her body.

When Mervet saw her friend Slim (a nickname given to him when he was heavy) at a party and asked how he lost so much weight, he told her he lost 60 pounds by training for a triathlon. Mervet wasn't sure she should attempt a triathlon, since she couldn't swim, but a co-worker assured her she could learn with the help of a training group.

Before she even considered a program, Mervet knew time would be a challenge. As a bank branch manager taking college courses, fitting swims, running, and biking into her busy schedule wouldn't be easy. Yet, she carved out time for training. She says, "You need to stay focused. Training may take away from other things, but you need to find the time to do it."

Mervet Joins TWT

Mervet joined Together We Tri (TWT) and continued challenging herself physically. She arrived at the first training session for the Chicago Sprint Triathlon, filled with doubt and wondering if she could ever succeed. Who did she think she was, trying to become a triathlete? She assumed this sport was reserved for super-human athletes, not normal people who wanted to live a healthy lifestyle and attain reasonable goals.

At first, Mervet couldn't swim a single length of the pool without stopping to catch her breath. She took her time progressing—adding laps to each workout and learning proper swim technique from Mary Bradbury, her coach with TWT. While cycling outside on the roads with the group, Mervet recalls stopping at a light, losing her balance, and falling. Her friend, Josh, who later heard about her fall, sent an email telling her not to worry, just keep getting back on her bike, because she was doing great. Mervet learned to keep riding, give her all each time, and not to worry about other athletes.

Coaches and other participants in the group taught her about pedal stroke, cadence, and shifting gears on her bike (more on this in a later chapter). With time, practice, and the proper training schedule, she felt more at ease with the group and with each sport. Each person in the group was caring and supportive; all helping her with her swims, bikes, and runs along the way. She often ran or cycled with friends from the group and rarely missed a weeknight or weekend TWT training session.

Mervet says, "Everyone in the group is here for a reason. Everyone has a story, and they're all inspiring."

During open water swim practices, Mervet and her friend Angie used the buddy system, making sure neither lost sight of the other. At

Mervet Ghbari

one of Angie's races she visualized the swim part of the race was just another practice at the Valley Lo Club lake, and Mervet was there practicing with her. Mervet felt great knowing that she, who didn't consider herself a swimmer, actually inspired and comforted someone else. Last year, a fellow athlete, Kim Morgan, walked Mervet to the swim start at one of their races; it really meant the world to her. The next year Mervet paid it forward and walked another woman to the swim start to lift her up.

Mervet's First Sprint Triathlon

Twelve weeks after enrolling in the program, Mervet accomplished her first triathlon—a sprint distance—and crossed the finish line crying tears of joy at her accomplishment. Her goal was to simply keep moving, not worrying about speed or time. She did keep moving and after the race she was on a high for weeks.

~~~~

Mervet is one example of ordinary people whose lives were changed by triathlons—not only the races, but also the training and friendship. Triathletes are not super-human. You can accomplish this, and much more, if you have the tools. Mervet pushed her limits and overcame her deepest fears. She's on a new path and a new lifestyle. You can be there with her.

Mervet:

66 Finishing my first tri was awesome! This challenge was more than physical—it was also about my family and culture. Growing up in a strict society, I was limited as to what I could and couldn't do. I never had a chance to discover what I'm capable of, or what I really like to do. I never thought I'd actually enjoy working out, let alone competing in triathlons. My mother was a firm believer in tough love and didn't show a lot of affection. Words of support and encouragement fell under the definition of affection in her dictionary; therefore, she didn't offer much of it. Competing in triathlons made me realize I can do anything. 99

Perhaps, like Mervet, you're stronger in one or two of the tri sports, or perhaps weak or strong in all three. If this is your first time combining all three, don't let thoughts such as, *I've never done it,* or *I don't know how* stop you. We all start from our own place and build our base, whether we're couch potatoes, marathoners, or nationally-ranked swimmers. No matter what your fears and hurdles, you too can become a triathlete and conquer your weaknesses.

Most of us ran as children, whether we played tag or ran bases. We rode bikes around the block and splashed in the pool. At some point in our lives many of us had fun with all three of the triathlon sports. Who ever thought about form? But form is exactly what you need to focus on when training for a triathlon. Correct technique will make you more efficient and save energy.

Consider how you stack up with the three sports. Have you always been a good runner and enjoyed it? Did you participate on a swim team and love to practice your strokes? Or were you the one who always wanted to ride bikes instead of walking? Triathlon training is a perfect opportunity to examine your abilities and where you may need to learn more about technique.

Before we consider the details of training, you need to recognize the importance of regularly training in your weak sport. You may be tempted to avoid swimming because it's tiring and your stroke is inefficient. Perhaps you'd like to skip cycling because you're skittish riding your bike on the road. Get it into your head that you'll need to train at least four days a week: two of those days in your weakest sport and one day a week in each of your stronger sports. If you can work out five days a week, you should devote two days to your two weakest sports and one toward your strong sport. If you're a go-getter, you may decide to do the six-day workout, which is two days a week per sport. The schedule is up to you. Listen to your body. Mix things up. You may find the energy for six workouts during one week, yet the next week you can barely manage the minimum of four. Don't sweat it. But remember you must take at least one rest day per week (we don't have to convince you, right?). And again, don't even think about skipping where you're weakest.

Now let's get to the heart of this chapter—improving your skills.

Make a Splash: Swim Your Best Stroke

Swimming is typically the most challenging of the three sports for beginner athletes, and most of us hate the thought of swimming in open water. Don't worry about this yet. The key for now is to practice, and then practice some more. Mary Bradbury, a swim coach for over 20 years and Team USA Member, 2006, 2009, and 2010, recommends taking lessons early on and working on your technique.

She says, "Efficiency is key! You want to come out of the water quickly, but with as much energy as you can for the bike and run. Improving technique is the only way to do so."

Mary Bradbury

If you practice swim technique, your body will thank you for the rest of your race. And don't enter a competition if you've only swum in a pool (unless the swim portion of the race is in the pool). Open water is a different thing altogether. The water is murky, the temperature is inconsistent, and no tidy swim lanes. You'll be surrounded by hordes of people with race anxiety (don't worry, after your training you won't be one of the anxious ones). In addition, you'll find no line on the bottom of the lake to guide you. To have a good race experience, you must practice swimming in open water and "sighting"—continuously checking if you're on course.

When Mervet began training, she could only float in the water. When she attempted to swim, she couldn't go a length without stopping to catch her breath. She'd never learned proper technique. Without it, swimming is horrifically inefficient and exhausting. With instruction from a certified TWT coach, plus regular practice and workouts, Mervet gradually improved. But swimming in the open water remained a huge hurdle.

Mervet was frightened to the point of tears the first time she had to swim in a lake, but her coaches promised she could do it. She could definitely handle the distance, and she'd worked hard on technique. This was about believing in her hard work and concentrating on her new stroke, while putting fear aside. First, Mervet swam a short distance to a buoy and back with her TWT training group. She was so shocked by her success she decided to swim further. With Libby's help, Mervet swam around two islands in the lake, totaling a half-mile. She swam part of the way with fear, and part with exhilaration. She progressed from barely being able to float to swimming a half-mile in open water. When she returned to the beach that day, she had a huge grin on her face. The group applauded her. This was a moment Mervet will always remember.

To build confidence in the water, let's review the three fundamentals of efficient swimming: balance, extension, and rotation.

Balance: Proper balance based on correct body positioning is the key to staying afloat. Frustrated swimmers often have poor positioning in the water, which leads to imbalance. Raising or flexing the neck to breathe instead of rolling your body and neck will throw off your body alignment, causing your hips and legs to drop and drag like a see saw; if one end is raised the other drops. To

Prone position, Mary Bradbury

visualize the correct position, imagine a straight rod running from the top of your head to your waist. Maintaining that position, roll your body and neck to catch a breath. When your lungs fill with air they become an internal buoy to help you displace water. Pressure on your "buoy" forces the water to push up your hips and keeps your legs from sinking.

Extension: Once you learn to properly balance your body, focus on extending your strokes and gliding. Contrary to common thought, short, quick, choppy, strokes won't get you to the other side of the pool faster. You need to extend, reach, and then pull through your swim stroke. Swim "tall" by elongating each stroke. Slow down while thinking, "Enter, extend, pause, and then pull." One way to practice this is to do front quadrant swimming (or FQS as first explained by swim expert Terry Laughlin in his book *Total Immersion: The Revolutionary Way*

Full extension with glide before stroke is taken, Mary Bradbury

to Swim Better, Faster, and Easier, Fireside, 1996), always having one arm extended and not starting a stroke until the second hand is visible in the front quadrant.

Rotation: Rolling from side to side with each stroke, rather than swimming flat, elongates your body, enabling you to glide further with less effort.

Breathing on each side can help you in rolling and is useful in choppy water.

The freestyle kick for endurance swimming is more for balance than for forward propulsion unless you're in an all-out sprint. In

Rotation with breathing, Mary Bradbury

the endurance swim during a triathlon your legs are more for balance, so kicking won't be a major part of your swim training. Don't waste too much energy on your kick. The freestyle flutter kick is generated at the hips and glutes, not the knee. Think of your legs as a whip initiating from the hips; your feet remain loose, slightly pointed, but not tense.

Hand entry is another swimming skill to fine-tune. Most Olympic swimmers' hands enter the water near the ear, with the thumb and forefingers first, pausing at full extension prior to starting their pull. When your hand enters the water, it should be positioned in front of the shoulder joint. Don't cross over the midline or your head when you enter or you'll snake from side to side rather than swim straight. During the pull phase, under water, your elbow should be high and your hand should pass over the midline of your body. While you're pulling through the water to finish your stroke, imagine pulling your body along a ladder, rung by rung, or that you're doing tricep extensions. Your elbow should exit the water first rather than the hand, or you'll end up "windmilling" your arm through the next stroke, which affects your balance.

High elbow technique, Mary Bradbury

In general, a slower stroke is a more efficient endurance stroke. The most efficient part of your stroke is when you're gliding just after your pull, so pause at the glide. Try to remember to say to yourself, "Enter, EXTEND, pause, and pull."

Once you develop an efficient stroke, you'll find the open water easier and less intimidating. Find a lake to practice in, but make sure you have a lifeguard or someone on dry land or in a boat to keep an eye on you. Ideally, you should practice mass starts, swimming close to other people and sighting. Sighting involves keeping an eye on a landmark or the swim exit spot so you don't go off course. In the race you won't be swimming in lap lanes. Believe me, you can add a lot of unwanted distance to your swim if you zigzag instead of taking a direct course. To sight in open water while you swim, practice quickly picking up your head and re-balancing to adjust your direction every three to five strokes. You can also sight when you take a breath. Breathe normally, then quickly look forward and peek at your course before dropping your head back to your balanced position and continuing your stroke. Bradbury suggests taking 15 to 20 strokes without sighting during a practice session, just to see where you end up. If you've veered off-course, try taking fewer strokes before sighting again to see where you are.

As you master the fundamentals of an efficient swim stroke, we recommend wearing a swim cap. It's mandatory on race day, so it's good to get used to wearing a cap during training. You'll receive a specific color swim cap to wear on race day, along with the rest of your wave.[1] Goggles are also a good idea; a quality pair of goggles isn't expensive, and the right pair can help with sun glare. Finally, for open water swims where the water is below 82 degrees Fahrenheit, you can wear a wetsuit. (If you wear a wetsuit when the water is warmer than 82 degrees, you'll be ineligible for any award.) If you can rent a suit and try it in the pool, you'll get the feel for the extra buoyancy and speed it provides. As we mentioned, a wetsuit keeps you warm but remember, you also have to peel it off during your transition. We'll discuss this in more detail during the transition chapter.

Pool IQ/Distance 101

If you are racing in a Sprint race your swim is a half mile. If you are racing in an Olympic race the distance is just shy of 1 mile.

---

[1] We'll have more information on wave starts and exactly what to expect on race day in the race week chapter

While you're training you will need to know how far you are swimming, so be consistent with counting your lengths/laps and recording your distances. You will also want to know if you are practicing in a 25 yard pool or a 25 meter pool.

- In a 25 yard pool: a half mile is 36 lengths, 1 mile is 72 lengths or 36 laps.
- In a 25 meter pool: a half mile is 32 lengths, 1 mile is 64 lengths or 32 laps.

Reading Your Swim Workout

(see sample swim workouts in the Appendix)

10 x 25 R20-30 means you swim 25 yards (one length of the pool from one side of the wall to the other) 10 times with 20-30 seconds of rest in between sets. The giant 60-second clock at the end of the lap lanes is a pace clock. Use this clock to time your rests and swims. If you're swimming with more than two people in a lap lane, circle-swim as follows: rather than swim from one side of the pool to the other in half of the lane (or taking up the entire lane), swim up on one side of the lane and down the other side; or swim counter-clockwise, always keeping the wall or lane line closest to your right as you swim. Let faster swimmers pass at the wall, and choose the lane most appropriate for your speed level.

Drills incorporate all the basic swim techniques and build on concepts from beginner drills to more advanced. It's important to do drills with each workout as you're developing your stroke; they are listed with your swim workouts. When doing each workout be sure to rotate through all the drills so you're working on all aspects for a perfect stroke.

In the Saddle: Finishing the Circle

During a triathlon, your swim in the lake is followed by a bike ride. You'll be on your bike, a little wet, riding for 12 miles if you're doing the sprint distance, and 24 miles if you're competing in the

Olympic distance. Feeling good and strong for this endurance ride is crucial to completing the triathlon's final piece: the run.

For now, during your first few weeks back in the saddle, find your comfort zone and get a feel for being on the bike. Don't worry if you don't own a fancy bike. Even if you have to dust off an old one and learn to ride again, no problem. Many first-time triathletes haven't ridden in years and get going again with whatever's available in the garage. If it has wheels, fits you, and is safe to ride, go for it. Get used to riding with a helmet, as they are mandatory in races—and rightly so.

Visit a local bike shop to check out triathlon bikes and get your bike tuned and fitted for you. A good fit is critical to prevent injuries and allows you to effectively use your muscles as you apply force to the pedals. Fit is also important to comfortable riding.

Follow these hints for a good bike fit:

1. **Saddle height:** Adjust the saddle (bike seat) so your hips don't rock during the pedal stroke and your knees don't bend more than 30 degrees. Measure your knee bend when your foot is at the bottom of the pedal stroke (6 o'clock position.

2. **Fore/aft saddle position:** To determine the proper position for your saddle, think of your pedal stroke as the circle of a clock and stop the pedals so your feet are in the three and nine o'clock positions. If your knees are too far forward over your ankles, your seat needs to be moved back (aft). If your knees are too far behind your ankles, your seat needs to be moved forward (fore). Your knees should be directly above your ankle in this "test" position for proper alignment.

3. **Handlebar reach:** There's no formula to determine the proper distance between your body and the handlebars. For this reason, be sure to test-drive a bike before buying it, making sure you don't feel too stretched out or that you are needing to reach too far when your hands rest on the handlebars. You should feel comfortable with your reach.

Most bike shops have expert bike fitters who can properly fit your current bike, or find and fit a new one. For the best fit, ride the bike more than once, practice shifting gears, and ask questions. Your bike is a great investment in your health, so choose it wisely.

Once your bike is fitted, ride with relaxed shoulders and a slight bend in your elbows. Don't lean on the handlebars; you'll put too much pressure on your hands, wrists, and elbows and may lose balance. Surprisingly, you'll use your core muscles to hold up your torso, so doing core strengthening exercises will benefit your riding.

For an efficient pedal stroke, push, then pull, in a circular motion. Think of pulling up on the bottom of the pedal stroke. Avoid pointing your toes downward during the pedal stroke, and keep your heel down to prevent numbness in your feet. Your pedal cadence— the number of times you complete a circle—should be between 80 and 100 repetitions per minute (rpms).

If you're nervous about riding on the open road, ride during low traffic times, avoiding rush hour. To simulate race day, we suggest riding with a group so you'll be accustomed to having other riders around you. Even if it's two or three friends, you'll learn to feel more comfortable having other athletes around you on the bike. Practice shifting while riding slowly, and experiment with the gears as you ride uphill, downhill, and on flat stretches. If you can, ride with a friend or expert who can give you tips and boost your confidence.

While starting out in this sport, the more support you can get the better, Don't let your self-doubt talk you out of your goal.

....

FAQs

1. ***When will my rear stop hurting?*** Time in the saddle, whether from frequent rides or long distances, will hurt your rear end. Wearing padded shorts can help, and some riders find relief by purchasing a gel seat. Keep working on an efficient pedal stroke and core strength, as this will place less body weight on your pubic area.

2. ***Why do my toes feel numb?*** Keeping your heel down and not pointing your feet down while riding will prevent numbness. Wiggle your feet and toes around in your shoes if you start feeling numbness during a ride, and make sure your shoes aren't too tight. If these hints don't help and you have clips, make sure your cleats are in the proper position. You may need to have them adjusted to make sure they are not placed on a pressure point causing nerve irritation.

3. ***Do I need aerobars?*** That depends on whether you're riding a road, mountain, or hybrid bike. If you're riding a mountain bike or hybrid bike, you don't need aerobars. The idea behind aerobars is to make you more aerodynamic. Aerobars help position you so there's less wind drag and you ride faster while racing. If you'll complete most of your training rides in busy areas, don't use the bars, because you'll need to access your brakes at all times and you can't do this quickly while using aerobars. As a beginner, it's difficult to balance and handle bars in the aero position, so it's best not to use them until you master your bike-handling skills. Take it slow while getting accustomed to the aero position.

Hit the Pavement: Find the Perfect Pace

Running is a simple sport that doesn't call for high-tech equipment. Almost anyone can run if they start from their own base and build appropriately. But people have different gaits and running styles, and form does matter if you want to become an efficient, faster runner.

Key take-away points for correct spinal alignment:

- head straight or leaning slightly forward,
- chin slightly tucked,
- chest upright and shoulders down,
- hips and butt forward and slightly tucked,

- arms comfortably bent, loose shoulders so arms can swing,
- feet should land on midsoles, then roll to front of foot,
- pick up heels after push-off,
- and most important, don't start out faster than your body and cardio are ready for. This will defeat you quickly.

This seems like a long list, but after you run often enough with proper body alignment, it'll come naturally. If running a mile seems like an eternity, break each session into doable walk-run-walk chunks.

Don't forget to warm up. Lacing up your shoes and taking off at break-neck speed isn't good for cold muscles or for new runner confidence. Spend the first five minutes of your run in a slow shuffle, gradually warming your muscles, then settle into a comfortable pace.

When you first start running and even if you've been running for a while, it's good to practice high cadence (how quickly you put down your feet). Over-striding when running is a common error. Your momentum slows when you plant the front leg too far out. A long stride also forces a heavy heel impact that can cause injuries. Focus on landing your foot under your center of gravity and taking shorter strides. Beginning runners can still shuffle with a high cadence and stay in their base training zone. To have an efficient 90 strike cadence, time yourself for one minute while counting each foot strike. Ideally, regardless of pace, this quick cadence shouldn't change.

Also, keep track of your time, no matter what it is, to give yourself an idea of your pace—how many minutes per mile you're running. Gradually increase your mileage by 10 to 15 percent per week, tapering every fourth week to give your body time to recover.

After each workout it's imperative to stretch while your muscles are warm, so you'll remain flexible and prevent injuries. Concentrate on stretching major muscle groups—your quadriceps, hamstrings, and calves. Also stretch the iliotibial (IT) band (actually fascia, not muscle), which runs along the outside of your thigh down to your knee. We'll show you some specific stretches in the next chapter.

Most important, you need a good pair of running shoes. You may have trouble parting with your trusty old athletic shoes, but a good, supportive shoe designed for running will make a world of difference to your body, providing essential stability, cushioning, and comfort. If you already own running shoes, take your last pair to a professional running store. Experienced staff can inspect the shoes' soles, analyze your gait, and then fit you with the most appropriate pair. If you have painful feet, see a podiatrist who can do an evaluation and possibly fit you with custom orthotics—special shoe inserts made specifically for your foot. They can do wonders if you have painful joints from past injuries, flat feet, or other common foot conditions.

Betsy: From Running to Triathlons

I ran my first 10K race with friends when I was in my 20s. I didn't know how to train properly, so I slowly increased my mileage until I was running six miles a few days before the race. During the race, miles five and six were especially tough, but what I recall most was my sense of accomplishment when I finished—plus the exhilaration of completing a race with fellow running enthusiasts. Energy and excitement surged around us as we drank bottled water and refueled with bananas and bagels. As we stretched, we swapped stories about the course. This first event led me to run other road races.

Then I moved out of the area. I stopped racing and fell into a rut, running three miles every time I went out, usually by myself. Eventually, I felt my body couldn't run more than three miles.

Finally, ten years and two sons later, I thought about racing again. I had more free time and noticed my community held numerous races— one that went right through my neighborhood. A friend who'd lost weight and was exercising every day told me she planned on doing a triathlon and asked my husband and I if we were interested. This seemed completely out of reach, but I couldn't help thinking it might be fun, and a great challenge. I discovered TWT was the perfect program for learning to prepare for a triathlon. I learned all about running from TWT coaches and ran further and faster than I ever dreamed possible. I discovered ways to improve my abilities and make running workouts fun.

Betsy:

❝I find running with a group is the most motivating way to train while having a great time. At the first group run with TWT, we increased our pace slowly with each lap. I found a runner about the same pace as me and we ended up playing cat-and-mouse, pushing each other to work harder. During another training session we did hill repeats with our coach. We ran hard up a hill, then jogged slowly down, sharing stories before the next hill. ❞

COACH TIP

Replace your running shoes every 300-500 miles.

COACH TIP

Drink about four ounces of water or sports drink every 15-20 minutes while running, and be sure to replenish your carbohydrate stores and electrolyte levels after each workout (more about refueling in the chapter on nutrition).

As you start your day-by-day tri training program outlined in this book, you'll build and fine-tune your skills. Just like Mervet, who started out learning to swim, ride, and run, you'll soon be able to compete in several sports.

Key Points

Take time to work on your skills for each sport and you'll be more efficient during training and faster on race day. Remember:

- *Swimming* — Balance, extension, and rotation are key. Practice sighting in open water.
- *Cycling* — Get your bike fitted. Complete a full circle when pedaling, keeping your heels down and your elbows relaxed.

Always wear a properly-fitted helmet, and work on gaining core strength.

- *Running* — Focus on correct body alignment. Purchase good-fitting, supportive shoes.

Stay relaxed and have fun!

CHAPTER 4

Play It Safe

"Our greatest glory is not in never falling,
but in rising every time we fall."
—Confucius

RUNNING AND EXERCISE became a part of Alice Chow's life when she celebrated her 40th birthday by committing to running a marathon within the next five to ten years. Until then, she was busy raising two children and couldn't find time to exercise. Alice embarked upon her plan by walking and jogging to build up endurance so she could walk/jog a 5K.

Alice Chow

The adventure began.

She continued entering 5K and 10K races, then at age 45 she ran a half marathon. She found a training group and ran her first Chicago Marathon at age 47.

Alice Chow

Following the marathon and winter training, Alice's feet began to feel tight and painful around the bottom and heels.

Alice:

66 I had no clue this was how plantar fasciitis felt. It was painful, but a blessing in disguise. I thought cross training would be better for my feet and when I learned about Together We Tri at the Glenview Park Center, I called Libby to ask if I could train for a triathlon with plantar fasciitis. She said, absolutely, and told me with a modified schedule I'd be stronger than ever at the end of training. She said I could run in deep water, swim, and bike with the group, while doing physical therapy. 99

Alice worked with a physical therapist to decrease her pain and strengthen her hip and quadriceps so she could remain injury free. She also used a foam roller on the bottom of her feet to work out the tightness by increasing blood flow to the area. Sometimes she massaged her foot and soaked it in warm water. Thanks to a great plan and a safe cross-training schedule, that summer Alice completed her first sprint triathlon. She was so elated at the finish line, she couldn't wait to do it all again the next year. Today, Alice is not only pain free, but a new woman. She triumphed over injury, gained strength, trained smart, and set her sights on new goals.

Alice learned her limits and now, at the first twinge of pain, she self-adjusts and takes precautions to keep her fasciitis in check. She says, "I believe in cross training to help prevent injuries and set new goals I never thought possible." Alice set a goal of completing an Olympic distance triathlon when she turned 50, and successfully did so that year in Chicago's triathlon—improving her miles per hour on the bike and feeling fabulous that she finished on a hot day. Her next goal? Shoot for a Half Ironman the next year.

Alice:

❝ When people ask me how my training progress is for any triathlon races, I tell them I am not "training" but rather the sports themselves have become part of what I do, a natural fabric of my life. As a mother and wife, my focus has been on taking care of family members and others. However, when I'm running, cycling, or swimming, I'm engaged in activities for myself. I treasure this personal sense of joy and fulfillment no one can possibly take away. As my running partner always says at the end of our run, "we are so blessed with our cups so full...we're ready to go out and spread the love. ❞

Listen to Your Body

If you ever experience an injury, learn from Alice: listen to your body, have an overall exercise plan that includes cross training for full body strength. You can train smart and prevent injuries that might otherwise derail your success. Play it safe and accomplish your goals.

With a core set of skills in your back pocket and the TWT training plan handy, you're almost ready to charge toward your first triathlon. First we'll share what experts and triathlon participants say about injury prevention and being safe on the road, in the water, and throughout your training.

First off, triathlon training goes hand in hand with cross training, since you'll be practicing three sports. This helps prevent injuries by strengthening muscle groups over your entire body. Don't be surprised if you feel a little twinge of pain here and there, flaring up at the oddest times. Let's face it, you'll be using that awesome body of yours more and more as you train slowly, increasing your mileage and distance. So let's be sure you listen to your body, treat yourself as you deserve, and stay smart about preventing injuries.

Injuries can happen to anyone at any time, especially if we overuse our bodies and train too much or too fast. We know you're excited about your new goals and you may want to jump in full force, but gradually building on your training will reap long term benefits. You'll have plenty of time for your body to adjust, gain strength, and recover as you build on your training. Twelve weeks is a safe time frame to build endurance and power for your race. And you will feel powerful.

Three months may not seem like much time to train, but you can transform yourself into an amazing triathlete in that amount of time. Keep following your safe training plan and just wait and see yourself at the end of this journey.

Betsy's toe:

66 Even young joints are injury prone. During college, while running with a friend on vacation (I hadn't been outside running in months), my left foot toe joint began hurting. This came out of nowhere—my joint suddenly became painful, then swollen. Being stubborn and naive, I iced it and went right back to running the next day. I should've listened to my body rather than ignoring the pain. I later learned I injured my joint because I have a limited range of motion in that toe. A podiatrist treated me with cortisone injection and orthotics. Ever since, I've had flare-ups from time to time. Now I listen to my body and immediately take care of aches and pains. 99

Together We Tri sticks by the 10 percent increase rule, meaning mileage is increased by 10 percent each week—a gradual progression to help prevent injuries. Slowly increasing your mileage weekly, along with planning for recovery and rest days, helps your body adapt to the demands of an endurance training program.

If at any time you feel overly fatigued or notice more aches and pains than usual, your body is telling you something. You'll benefit from taking an extra rest day or two rather than muscling through a workout when your body asks for recovery time. Don't stress over missing a workout here and there. You'll have plenty of time to catch up. Everyone is different, so learn to adjust and train for *you*.

As you begin your tri journey, it's crucial to recall any previous injuries and weaknesses, so you can take measures to avoid re-injuring yourself. Be aware of personal areas that are susceptible to injury and take precautions to sideline them as quickly as possible. During the program you'll also keep track of your perceived exertion, mileage, and how you're feeling overall.

Typically, most injuries can be prevented by paying attention to your body — catching symptoms early, and taking time off to rest.

We should expect a little discomfort and muscle soreness with pushing ourselves. Anytime you use muscles you don't normally fatigue, you'll feel some soreness. But what we really don't want is pain that is severe and persistent. This pain will be different from sore muscle discomfort. If you feel true pain, then listen to your body and rest, or slow down your pace of workouts.

If you miss workouts because of pain, or even a busy schedule, don't try to make up the time. Let it go and don't fret. If you try to fit in a missed workout on a rest day, you are not *safely* following the plan. Adding another rest day is better than adding an unplanned workout. If you miss a scheduled workout and can swap it with a rest day, that's great. But if you can't find the time, let it go and don't worry.

RICE it!

We're not talking about jasmine rice, but rather the first aid treatment for muscle injuries: REST, ICE, COMPRESS and ELEVATE. For injuries, the best thing you can do is quickly RICE the area to decrease inflammation (swelling), relieve pain, and protect tissues. If symptoms persist, see your doctor to have the area examined. The last thing you want is to work through the pain and miss something serious you could've resolved early on.

Stretching—a must!

Stretching tends to be the most overlooked component of training, yet is one of the most important. Be sure to include a flexibility and stretching component to all your workouts. Make sure to stretch the whole body and hold each stretch for at least 20 seconds. Do your stretches after your muscles are warmed up and your blood is flowing. Include a five minute warm-up involving a slow run, cycle, or swim, at the beginning of each workout (as per

IT/gluteal stretch
Alice Chow

the training program). These warm up distances still count toward your total mileage. Believe us, your tempo or track work and your cycling intervals will feel better after

Calf stretch, Julie Schultz

Hamstring stretch
Libby Hurley

you've had a slow warm up. Never stretch cold muscles, as you may cause an injury to a tight muscle that hasn't been adequately warmed up.

Strength training wisdom

Triathlon is an endurance event, so you'll need strength training to help you succeed in the each sport. Strengthening

Neck stretch
Libby Hurley

through weight lifting and core work is extremely important, because it helps prevent injuries and increase joint stability. Pay special attention to strengthening your large muscle groups, as well

Quadricep stretch
Libby Hurley

as hip, pelvic, abdominal, and low back muscles; these core supportive muscles not only give stability, but also help you perform. If you are currently on a light strength or resistance program, then by all means continue. We recommend strength training 2-3 times a week. A short session after a run or swim works well, but you can fit it in where ever you like. However, we don't recommend strength training before an intense swim, bike, or run workout.

Jennifer Fox, physical therapist and certified strength and conditioning specialist with Athletico is on the medical staff for the USA Triathlon team. She says, "Triathletes move in a forward direction and are subject to repetitive overuse. Training smart will help deter you from experiencing injuries. Athletes who don't know how to train properly are more likely to get injured." Fox suggests strength training with lighter weight resistance and more repetitions to build strength for endurance.

You don't need fancy weight equipment for strength training. Use your own body weight, either indoors or out on a small patch of grass.

Sample Workout:
- lunges
- push-ups
- squats
- dips
- abdominal curls
- low back extension ("superman")

Two sets of 12 to 15 repetitions makes a good starting point. If you're strength training more frequently and using heavier weights, put this workout aside until the off-season. This is not the time to break your bench press weight record.

Lunge, Libby Hurley

Push up, Libby Hurly

Modified push up, Libby Hurley

Dips for triceps, Libby Hurley

Squats, Alice Chow

Abdominal crunch, Libby Hurley

Low back extension, Libby Hurley

COACH's TIP

"Make sure to train in all disciplines, (swim, bike, run) during the week, allow for adequate recovery time, and remember to taper your training before a race."

-Jennifer Fox, PT, CSCS

Common Injuries

Swimming injuries

Shoulder Impingement Syndrome: Tissue damage and pain occurs when the rotator cuff tendon is pinched as it passes through the front shoulder. This is most common in females and people with flexible joints.

Take Action: Focus on your swim form; rotate your trunk with each stroke and use correct arm movement to help keep your shoulders in good working shape. Shoulders will gradually get stronger. Stretching pectorals (shoulder muscles) and lats (upper back muscles) after a swim workout will help prevent pinched tendons.

Neck Pain: Don't let swimming be a pain in the neck. Improper head position while swimming long distances can cause pain from over extending your neck.

Take Action: Try not to look up while swimming, but instead keep your gaze down at the bottom of the pool lane or lake (which usually is murky). Since you'll have to sight while open water swimming, once you lift your head to sight ahead, go right back to your straight swim position—as if a rod passes from the top of your head to your pelvis. Remember to rotate around the rod.

Low Back Pain: Over-extending the back while swimming may cause low back pain.

Take Action: Again, don't look up too much when taking a breath while swimming, but position your head with your forehead down and in the water. Tightening your buttocks and abdominal muscles will help control loose abdominals and exaggerated arch of the spine as well as over-rotation of the shoulders and pelvis, which may cause low back pain.

Bicycle injuries

Knee Injuries: You'll be powering through the miles on your bike, and repetitive rotations can cause overuse to the ilio-tibial (IT) band. You'll know where it is if you feel the strain. The IT band is the band of fascia on the outer lower aspect of the knee.

Take Action: A well-fitted bike along with slowly increasing mileage will help avoid knee issues as you build strength. Again, stretch and strengthen the area if you begin to feel pain.

Neck Pain: Let's face it—sitting on a bike is not the most natural and comfortable position. As you lean forward with hands on your bike's handlebars and brakes, keeping your eyes forward and focused on the road may cause neck and shoulder pain.

Take Action: Too far a reach can lead to nerve injuries. Believe us, a slight adjustment is worth it. Take periodic posture breaks where you sit up on your seat and tuck your chin into your chest to relieve muscle tension in your neck.

Low Back Pain: Sitting for hours hunched (flexed) over on a bike is hard on your lower back. Be sure not to "hunch" too much while riding.

Take Action: Take a break and stretch your back by sitting straight on the seat of your bike and arching your back. Since your hips and legs are connected to your back, take a few minutes during a break to stretch your hips, glutes, quads, and hamstrings.

Betsy' Bike Fit:

66 Before buying my Trek Madone WSD (Women's Specific Design) bike I had a chance to take it on a long ride - actually on a week-long cycling trip down the coast of California. While riding for hours on my borrowed road bike (the longest mileage I've ever ridden) I gradually felt tingling in my left arm and wrist. Frankly, it scared me. I told our guide, who knew right away my bike needed adjustment. The discomfort was completely relieved once he repositioned my seat and handlebars. Proper fit does make a difference. 99

Running injuries

Ilio Tibial (IT) Band Syndrome is a common complaint of triathletes because of repetitive running and cycling. Increasing mileage, hill running, track running, or weak hip muscles all contribute to an angry, inflamed IT band. "Improper cleat float may cause improper alignment of your leg, leading to inefficient or incorrect pedal stroke, causing ITB issues," notes Fox. "Be careful to make sure you're in the proper gear when riding your bike. If the gear is too high, it can cause you to push too hard on the down stroke."

Prevention: RICE the area and take time off if the pain doesn't give up. Anti-inflammatory meds will also help bring down the swelling. Check your running shoes to see if they're breaking down and watch boosting your mileage too soon. Fox suggests hill runs are good for variance—they'll make you stronger and help prevent injuries because you use your hamstrings on the uphill run and quads on the downhill. It's good to train opposite muscle groups to balance muscles as you continue gaining strength.

Julie Schultz

Only a few weeks away from her first tri race (Danskin), Julie, a Glenview, Illinois mom, was ramping up to run six miles while visiting Galena, Illinois. "While running in a hilly area, I felt intense pain around my knee. It was killing me, but I didn't stop. Turns out, I irritated an old injury from years ago and then limped around and cried about it." The lesson: "If you're in pain, stop and listen to your body," says Julie. She did therapy—strength building for her IT band—and had to bow out of her first triathlon, but was still able to cycle and swim. She gradually built up to running three miles in time for her official first tri; the Chicago Triathlon in late August. She felt great and was smiling during the entire race.

Julie was smart about her injury and took care of it in time so she was still able to have a successful season. Injuries can become chronic and debilitating if not addressed in time.

Julie Schultz

Shin Splints: Sore shin muscles (mid to lower anterior leg) are usually felt at the start or end of exercise and feel bruised when touched. It's difficult to even walk, yet sometimes the pain subsides when running. Better always to be safe than sorry and RICE.

Prevention: Back off on your running mileage, forget hill runs for a while, and stretch your calves. Doing toe raises, foot circles, and heel walking will strengthen your shins. If pain persists, see a physician to rule out a stress fracture.

Plantar Fasciitis: Painful first steps in the morning right out of bed are a sign of plantar fasciitis. Pain in the heel and bottom of the foot is a runner's menace. Take care of this quickly, as it can be persistent during your training if ignored.

Prevention: RICE, along with regular massage of the arch with a tennis ball. Regular calf and Achilles stretches are also beneficial. Check the wear of your shoes and consider custom molded orthotics to give your foot the proper arch support.

Julie:

66 I had 4 children in 4 years. I felt blessed to have been able to have healthy children, but those years were long and tiring. They were also pretty selfless. When my fourth child was 4 months old I decided it was time to get my body back. I started really watching what I ate and running 5 days a week as I did before I had my children. The weight came off and I got stronger. However, about 6 months later I was in a funk. Doing the same thing every day had put me in a rut. And during this time, my 2-year-old daughter had been diagnosed with an autoimmune disease that threw me for a loop. There was no doubt about it; I was feeling very down even during my runs. As often happens, the answer came to me in a way I hadn't imagined. My friend Ellen called me and told me she had signed up for a triathlon training program. I had missed the first session, but I could join

Bike safety

ALWAYS WEAR A HELMET!

- Don't listen to your MP3 player while cycling.
- Adhere to traffic laws, especially stop signs and traffic signals.
- Use arm signals to show cars which direction you're turning. Never glide through an intersection.
- Before passing another cyclist, call out "On your left!"
- Make sure your clips aren't too tight so you don't get stuck in them at an intersection.
- Never stop in the middle of a road or path. Pull over to the side as far as you can before stopping.
- Be careful when passing parked cars. Look in the side mirror to see if anyone is in the car, ready to open the door.
- Wear reflective clothing if you're cycling at dawn, dusk, or dark.

in on the next and work out for 12 weeks while learning how to complete a triathlon. I spoke to my husband about it, and he didn't hesitate in telling me to go for it. I had always wanted to compete in a triathlon after seeing my brother do it years ago, but didn't know where to start. I couldn't even imagine this would be the answer I'd been looking for to get me out of the dumps. I got so much out of it that I had never expected. Besides lifting my mood, I finally had something that was MINE, and it felt as if I had discovered a new passion. I was surprised and so pleased to discover the sessions with my fellow triathletes were actually as fun and uplifting as the actual race, once I did complete one. The kinship I discovered with the other members and coaches was just incredible. They are wonderful women I feel so blessed to have met and befriended. To this day I made connections with people I know will be my comrades for life. 🙶

Open water safety

- NEVER SWIM ALONE. Take a buddy on your swim to keep an eye on you in case you get tired or have cramps. Unexpected things can happen and you don't want to be swimming in open water without help when you need it. The best safety tip is to have someone in a kayak or canoe next to you while you swim.
- Check the weather forecast before suiting up. Storms can approach quickly and you don't want to be caught miles away from shore when thunder rumbles or lightning strikes.

Running safety

- Wear reflective gear when running at night
- Don't crank up the volume on your MP3 player. You'll still need to hear oncoming cars and other walkers, runners, and cyclists.
- If you haven't been running, it's not wise to begin with trail runs or lots of hills. Gradually work up to these as recommended in the training guide.

Key Points

Follow the 10 percent rule of increasing your mileage 10 percent each week. Don't do too much, too fast.

- Be sure your gear fits properly.
- Stretch and strengthen regularly.
- If you do get an injury, RICE it. See your physician if pain persists.
- Journal in your TRI Notes on your progress and any aches.

CHAPTER 5

Boost Your Energy

*"Destiny is not a matter of chance, it is a matter of choice.
It is not a thing to be waited for, it is a thing to be achieved."*
—William Jennings Bryan

NANCY HURST BROKE INTO THE triathlon scene in 1994, when a friend coaxed her into signing up for a tri without any training or idea of what she was doing.

Nancy Hurst

Nancy did two sprint triathlons before registering for the biggest triathlon in the world, the Chicago Triathlon (at the time named Ms. T's triathlon). "I swam in a regular full-piece bathing suit and didn't wear goggles. Once I got out of the water, I put on cotton shorts, a tank top, and hopped onto my mountain bike." Nancy laughed. "For two summers I did a few triathlons here and there, then stopped and began to run marathons, completing a total of five."

Only after signing up for the all-women's Together We Tri training program in 2004 at her city gym club did Nancy learn how to train for a tri the right way—a move that changed the entire sport for her.

"Tris were a lot of fun for me, but I'd missed out on the experience of training hard for something and completing a goal. With the women's training group, it changed into something bigger. Completing a triathlon after putting my heart and soul into training for 12 weeks gave me a different perspective. I learned there are no limits, and if I work hard at something I can accomplish it and have fun along the way. I met some of my closest friends from day one and really enjoyed the challenge and getting better at it."

After that, Nancy kept on going—completing Sprint, Olympic, and then a Half Ironman distance triathlon. She

Nancy Hurst

soon realized each race is different. During her half ironman (1.2 mile swim, 56 mile bike, 13.1 mile run, which usually takes six or more hours for an amateur), Nancy faced unexpected circumstances and struggled to meet her body's fuel demands. The race was held on a hot, steamy July day at Racine, Wisconsin's Half Ironman, 2008. Nancy's bike rack and gear was all set up when she headed for the starting line and learned the race's start time had changed. "Our start was delayed by one hour because of fog, so my nutrition was off from the beginning," says Nancy. Then, to top it off, the course drink of the day (provided by the race sponsor) wasn't what she was accustomed to. It didn't sit well in her stomach. Nothing else besides water was available on the course.

On her bike she carried one bottle of water and one bottle of Gatorade, which she drank early on. She drank another two bottles of water while on the 56 mile course, but didn't have any more electrolytes with her. Nancy headed into the bike-to-run transition

(T2), put on her running shoes, and started the 13.1 mile course. She stopped to drink water at every hydration station and took in only a few gels with carbs and electrolytes.

Immediately after her race finish, Nancy started feeling light headed and a little woozy. She tried to eat a banana and bagel, but nothing felt good going down. She hung out at the race site for over an hour, talking to other racers and friends, taking photos, and even dipping back into the lake. However, she continued to feel worse. In hindsight, Nancy wishes she'd gone to the medical tent to be checked out. Instead, she loaded her car with her gear and started back home with Libby. She didn't take seriously the fact that she was feeling bad. After all, she'd just completed a Half Ironman.

When Nancy and Libby (also a race participant) stopped to eat, Nancy felt lightheaded and nauseous. Libby recognized that Nancy was low on electrolytes and sprinkled salt in her mouth and put a soda up to her lips, but it was too late. Nancy started shivering and felt nauseated. Libby took her to the emergency room where she received four bags of fluids to replenish dangerously low sodium levels.

Fluid imbalance can be insidious, as it sneaks up on you with few initial symptoms. More often than not, by the time you start to feel thirsty, fatigued, or dizzy, you're already way behind in fluids. You may not realize it, but we even sweat when we're swimming, losing mainly sodium and potassium. Following your hydration plan is especially important on the long course.

Nancy says, "It's so important to stay ahead of your carbs and fluids and not wait until you're thirsty or hungry. By then it's too late." In hindsight, she says it would have been a good idea to experiment with a sodium supplement on her long training. Proper nutrition is key to feeling prepared and strong on race day.

You should also have a nutrition plan for your race. You'll stay ahead of yourself by taking in fluids or carbs every 20 minutes, keeping a steady balance of energy in your system. With these simple guidelines, you'll feel energetic during the race and finish strong.

Nancy:

66 I have done things I never thought possible. I learned about what I am capable of and how I can do just about anything I set my mind to. Triathlons have empowered me in such a deep way. It is never about the time or place I finish; it's always about doing the best I can and knowing no one can take that away from me. 99

Before her Madison, Wisconsin Ironman in September 2010, Nancy sent an email to family and friends:

66 This has been a long journey and I hope on race day I can relax and enjoy the experience. I know it will be physically and mentally painful and challenging, but I also hope I can take away from the day an even deeper appreciation of what I have, what I am capable of doing and that I am fully supported by family and friends. I know I could not have done this without Brian (husband). He has supported me from the day I set out to do this. I feel we worked together to make it happen. I am hoping to cross that finish line on Sunday and feel pride. If I am unable to cross the finish line then I hope I have the courage to try again another time. 99

Nancy did complete the Ironman successfully!

As you challenge your body to perform in each of the tri sports, always be mindful of the need for fuel. Your body will carry you across the finish line: take care of it and keep it running efficiently with the right balance of nutrients. For endurance sports, proper nutrition means as much as physical training. We'll show you the essentials so you know what you need for training and your race day plan.

Your nutrition experiences make a great feature for your journal. As you train, keep track of what works for you and what doesn't rest well on your stomach, so you'll know exactly what you need on race day. If you can pinpoint your nutrition plan for race day you can actually cross the finish line with extra umph in your step, rather than feeling depleted and staggering across the line.

During the tri journey, your awareness of your body's reaction to exercise and increased training will heighten. You'll think more about what you eat and what your body needs, because you'll be demanding more of your body, committing to swim, bike, and run more frequently. Throughout the TWT program, your body will gradually transform—improving your cardiovascular system and muscular endurance—and you'll need to adjust your nutrition plan accordingly. Keeping your tank fueled and hydrated before, during, and after each workout session and race is critical. If you neglect this, you may find yourself too exhausted to build on your last workout.

Fueling for Your Workout

From day one of your training program you'll need food that sits well in your stomach; food that's easily digestible and won't cause issues as you work out. Eating before exercise will help improve your performance, since food tops off muscle and liver glycogen stores that provide our muscles with fuel, thereby increasing muscle energy. As a result, you'll be able to exercise longer and with greater intensity without feeling fatigued. In your new athlete's diet, aim for 60 percent of calories from carbohydrates, 10 to 15 percent from protein, and 25 to 30 percent from fat.

Carbohydrate munchies

Grains, fruits, vegetables and dairy are all high carb foods.

We recommend you snack on:

- 2 slices of bread
- 1 cup grapes
- 1 apple
- 8 crackers
- 1 cup yogurt with fruit

Deb Ognar, RD, and Certified Specialist in Sports Dietetics, says, "Everyone has their own tolerance level when it comes to foods. Foods that work best will vary from person to person, so try simple foods anywhere from one to four hours before a workout to see how you feel. Take smaller amounts of food if you'll be exercising one hour later, while a larger meal is fine if you'll be exercising within three or four hours."

Athletes should focus on consuming carbohydrates and fluids, says Ognar, because these foods are easily digested and rapidly used by your body for immediate energy. But, since they're rapidly used when you exercise, you need to keep filling your body with quick fuel sources to feed your muscles during strenuous workouts. Clif Shot Bloks, Gatorade, and Jelly Belly sport beans are a few we've tried. If you're sensitive to caffeine, pay attention to the caffeine content in each energy bar, bean, gu/gel, or blok. Some gels have twice the caffeine of others and it may affect you.

Follow this formula to determine the amount of carbs you need about an hour before exercising:

Light to moderate training:
5-7 grams of carbs per kilogram of body weight
(1 kg = 2.2 lbs)

Heavy training to high intensity:
7-10 grams of carbs per kilogram of body weight
Example: a 150 pound person should shoot for 475-680 grams of carbs.

Good options to eat 1 to 2 hours before a workout:
- bagel and peanut butter + banana + fluids
- turkey sandwich, cup of pasta, veggies and a banana
- cereal with milk + a piece of fruit
- yogurt + fruit
- energy bar + fruit

NUTRITION COACH TIP

"Choose easily digestible food before you work out. Be cautious about eating high fiber foods that will stay with you longer and tend to create gas. Protein will also stick with the body longer, giving you a sustained (not as immediate) fuel and energy source."

-Deb Ognar, RD

Did you know?

The body stores enough glycogen for 90-120 minutes of exercise.

Libby's fuel tips

While you're on your bike, this is the easiest time to refuel your body and eat much needed solid foods. I like Clif Shot Bloks and typically eat one or two every 30 minutes while I'm cycling, depending on how I feel. I always keep two water bottles on my bike, one filled with water and the other with an electrolyte drink. I alternate a few gulps every 15 minutes while riding. Be sure you practice drinking while riding, because this is your prime time to take fluids. While you're on the run, drink every mile at a water station, alternating between Gatorade and water.

Get your fuel on!

With the TWT Sprint training plan you'll start with shorter training sessions, moving toward longer sessions with brick workouts (back to back work outs, swim to bike or bike to run). The Olympic distance training schedule incorporates longer workouts earlier in the schedule to build endurance. By longer, we mean over 60 minutes of continual exercise. During these longer sessions, even though your body has adapted, you'll need to hydrate regularly and fuel to replenish your glycogen stores, providing energy to muscles that are broken down and rebuild as you grow stronger through your training.

We suggest trying different sports beverages, gels, gu's, and Shot bloks that contain a balanced amount of carbs, sodium, potassium, and fluids to quickly restore what you've used during early parts of your workout. Ideally, you should consume 100 calories during every 30 minutes of exercise, either through food or liquid.

Hydration smarts

- Before Exercise: Two hours, drink 14 - 22 oz of fluids
- During Exercise: Drink 6 - 8 oz. every 15 to 30 minutes.
- After Exercise: Aim to drink 16 - 24 oz. for every pound lost during exercise.

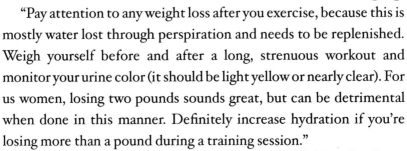

COACH TIP

"Pay attention to any weight loss after you exercise, because this is mostly water lost through perspiration and needs to be replenished. Weigh yourself before and after a long, strenuous workout and monitor your urine color (it should be light yellow or nearly clear). For us women, losing two pounds sounds great, but can be detrimental when done in this manner. Definitely increase hydration if you're losing more than a pound during a training session."

~Coach Mary Bradbury
Together We Tri Trainer

Your urine should be light colored NOT dark!

DANGER ZONE: Signs of dehydration:

- light headedness,
- lack of energy,
- dizziness,
- fatigue,
- decrease in appetite/nausea,
- dark yellow or amber urine.

The longer term consequences of dehydration include intestinal upset, problems with concentration, low blood volume, and rapid heart rate.

Betsy's First Olympic Tri

On the warm August morning of the 2008 Chicago Triathlon, I felt calm and ready to race. I thought I'd followed the TWT plan perfectly, eating a banana and juice for breakfast (I should have eaten oatmeal or cereal, too) and carrying gels and sports beans for my transitions. Two bottles were on my bike cages: a sports drink and water. The transition closed at six a.m, but my wave didn't start until 8:48 a.m. Off I went, and grabbed a gel at the swim-to-bike transition. While I was on the bike for over an hour, the temperature slowly rose. Empty water bottles littered Lake Shore Drive. I swerved to dodge some of them on my way. I thought, *focus and don't lose your balance or else I'll hit a bad spot and get a flat.*

As I passed other athletes and they passed me, I sipped only a little bit of my drinks and realized later I should have taken a lot more. More than a few cyclists struggled, replacing flat tires on the side of the road. I came into the bike-to-run transition (T2) feeling good. The heat and humidity continued to build, and I could feel it on the six mile run. I grabbed drinks at the water stations, but at about the three mile turn around, it hit me ... extreme thirst. I remember looking at my watch and feeling surprised it was after 11 a.m. I stopped again at one of the stations, where I stood and drank Gatorade. The lime taste burst into my dry mouth and I couldn't get enough. I was already dehydrated and trying to get in as much fluid as possible. I still had some miles to run, so I kept my legs moving as I saw the finish line and my family cheering me on. I heard the announcer call my name, and a moment later I crossed the finish line, holding both arms in the air.

I took the cold, wet towel a volunteer handed me and sucked on it, then headed to the drink table for more. I was caught up in the moment of the race, then, seeing TWT friends, and getting my stuff out of transition. I finally did eat a bagel and banana, since we had a long walk back to transition to our bikes, wetsuits, and gear bags. While in a sub shop with my family a few hours after my finish, I began feeling nauseous. My blood sugar dropped suddenly while waiting in line. I quickly got food in and slowly felt better. I was borderline disaster.

It's good to be cautious on your bike, but you still need to drink often. You'll be excited when you finish, but remember to fuel, drink, and take in even more fuel immediately after your race. You'll feel so much better as you celebrate your journey.

Sweat Facts

You lose sodium (an electrolyte) when you sweat. Electrolytes help regulate blood pressure, blood volume, muscle contraction, nerve impulses, and cellular fluid levels. During hot, humid conditions, the body may lose up to 20 quarts of fluid per day. That's why adequate sodium intake is imperative for your body to function normally, much less race.

After you sweat: après workout fuel

As you swim, cycle, run—or perform any combination of two of these sports—you'll deplete most of your glycogen stores and need to quickly fill your tank. Your body is efficient and your muscles are ready to take in additional carbs, but this process is more efficient if you properly refuel. Ognar emphasizes that athletes have a 30 minute window after exercise to eat and restore energy to muscles, which will result in a higher storage of glycogen and hence a quicker recovery and readiness for the next challenge. In other words, it's best to eat soon after you cool down and stretch. Ognar suggests the following foods to eat after a workout:

Post workout food options
- 2 handfuls of pretzels + string cheese + 8 oz. of sports drink,
- 12 oz. of chocolate milk + low fat granola bar,
- 20 oz. Gatorade + sports bar,
- Shakes such as Ensure, Boost, or Muscle Milk.

Protein is an essential nutrient for an athlete's diet. Controversy exists as to whether protein is essential for exercise recovery, but the amino acids in protein are known to help repair and build muscles. In general, 10 to 15 percent of an athlete's diet should come from protein. Let's face it, one of our goals is to gain muscle as we lose excess fat, and adding protein after a workout has been proven to help with these goals.

Protein Sources

- meat,
- chicken ,
- fish,
- eggs,
- dairy,
- beans.

Shedding a Few Pounds

Getting trim and fit is a common goal for many women who decide to train for a triathlon. Why not? You'll be exercising five to six days a week, so naturally you'll expect to lose fat and gain muscle. But keep in mind you'll be hungry and you need to eat enough to keep going. Ognar recommends you focus on weight loss during the early part of training, rather than the later part when the intensity and duration of your workouts lengthen and hunger increases. If you restrict calories, you risk not consuming enough calories for energy when you need to perform. And if you don't consume your daily requirements, you'll be more susceptible to illness and injury. Follow these guidelines when it comes to dropping pounds while training.

- Get valuable high nutrient carbs in while cutting back on high fat foods (less salad dressing, mayonnaise, etc).
- Limit alcohol and sweets.
- Cut as many processed foods as possible.
- Focus on whole grains, cereals, low-fat dairy products, fruits and vegetables — these pack in nutrients.

Eating smaller, frequent meals and snacks each day improves your body's use of energy.

Healthy fats are essential

- unsaturated oils,
- fish,
- nuts,
- seeds,
- avocado.

Calories burned based on a 135 pound woman

- 100 calories per mile of running,
- 600 calories per hour of swimming,
- 500 calories per hour of biking.

To maintain your current weight, eat 15 times your body weight in calories, and then add calories burned during exercise. If you weigh 150 pounds and run 10 miles one day, you need to eat (15x150) + (10x100) = 3,250 calories. If you want to lose a few pounds, then eat a little less than the amount needed to maintain your weight.

These are generalizations, and exact calorie burning is different for each of us, depending on weight, height, and effort. In general, every 10 minutes of moderate exercise swimming, biking, or running, will burn 100 calories.

Get Some ZZ's

Whether you awaken by five or six in the morning to squeeze in your exercise for the day or go out to run a few hours after dinner, you need to sleep a full seven to eight hours a night.

We get it. Often it's impossible to fit in exercise AND get adequate amounts of sleep. Do your best while training to treat yourself well and get your rest. Your body needs to rejuvenate and restore so you can go for it again the next day. Harvard researchers at Brigham and

Women's Hospital note that depriving ourselves of sleep will affect health, fitness, and weight.

Lack of sleep can wreak havoc with hormones that regulate appetite, causing you to crave high-calorie, fatty foods—not what we want to eat while trying to transform ourselves and become strong, sleek, lean, and mean fat burning machines. Adequate sleep becomes even more important as your activity levels increase with the TWT plan.

Race Day Fuel

If you follow your TWT training guide to the best of your ability, you'll have training down to a science before race day, along with a fine-tuned personal nutrition plan. You'll know exactly what works for you and what does not.

As Nancy discovered, unforeseen things can happen on race day, so it's imperative you be prepared, but also be flexible and able to make changes while you're competing. Always think on the course and consider nutrition as you train and race. Although you'll simulate race day by doing bricks and a mini-tri (see Chapter 11), you never *really* know what to expect until race day arrives. Nerves will likely kick in, but in general, your body's requirements will be the same on race day as for your longer workouts.

Follow these tips and you'll be ready on race day.

- Look into which products are offered on the race course and try them in training. Not being familiar with the on-course fuel can mess with you mentally and physically. You may lose one of your own sports drinks and need to rely on what's available.
- DON'T EAT ANY NEW FOODS the morning of the race or the evening before.
- Eat easily digestible foods that are low in fiber.
- Bring a banana, a piece of bread, or a bagel to eat about 15 minutes before the race.

Key Points

1. Be sure to fuel up before you work out. Eat a larger meal 3 to 4 hours before exercising and a light snack 1 to 2 hours before.

2. Keep a steady balance of fluids and carbs in your system as you train and race.

3. Hydrate, hydrate, hydrate! Before, during, and after exercise.

4. Eat carbohydrates within 30 minutes after exercising.

5. Have a race day nutrition plan in place and practice it during training.

6. Aim for 60% of calories from carbs, 10 to 15% from protein, and 25 to 30% from fat.

7. Eat high quality foods; avoid sugar and alcohol.

8. Get some ZZZ's! Sleep is a vital part of your training.

9. Don't eat anything new on race day.

SECTION II

You Can Become an Athlete

NOTES

CHAPTER 6

Use Your Training Guide

*"You are never given a dream without also being
given the power to make it come true."*
-Richard Bach

ON A MILD TUESDAY evening in mid-April, Karen Kurkowski
sat in a room with women eager to start their first day of training.

Karen Kurkowski

When Karen heard the others tell stories of their athletic
endeavors, her heart rate quickened. "I was panic stricken when the
women introduced themselves. Some had even run marathons. I had
no tri gear—not even a sports bra!" says Karen, a stay-at-home mom
of three. Karen admits she felt like a "nobody" while she sat next to
her friend Ellen, who encouraged her to attend the initial meeting.
Up until then, Karen's activities had all been family oriented.

Libby saw concern in Karen's eyes, so when the group headed
outside for a run, Libby stayed by Karen's side the entire way, telling
her she could do it by putting one foot in front of the other, moving
forward, and not going faster than a casual pace to start. Karen and
Libby ran 30 slow minutes together, and Libby told her not to push

Karen Kurkowski

her pace saying, "If you feel too winded to talk, lets walk a couple of minutes and then start again. Today is day one. You don't need to run the full three miles at race pace. You're exactly where you should be right now. This is stepping stone one and we'll build slowly. Just listen to your body and I promise, if you stick to the training, you'll be running five miles before you know it."

Karen kept running.

At 6:30 a.m. the following Sunday, Karen stood at the side of the pool, again feeling uneasy. She didn't know how to swim and couldn't do a single lap in a pool. As the Together We Tri coach began teaching her the fundamentals that morning—balance, rotation, and breathing—Karen worked hard on her stroke. Week after week she added laps, and gradually she was swimming eight laps, then 16. (*With any sport, learning the fundamental and proper technique is where you need to start. No need to build countless laps on a poor stroke. So we always focus on drills and getting it right at the beginning.*)

Karen kept attending the group training sessions and following the training plan on her own each week, with a goal to complete the Glenview Park Center Triathlon at the end of July. She still lacked confidence, but felt herself gradually progressing from day to day. She was getting stronger and running farther.

Before training for a triathlon, Karen had lost 35 pounds after her daughter was born (her third child) by walking two miles a day and eating only 1,200 calories a day. She wanted to keep her weight off and was going through a stressful time when her friend reached out to her to try triathlon training with Together We Tri. Karen knew she needed to take the next step to get stronger and healthier.

The Together We Tri training plan was easy for Karen to follow. She kept a positive attitude with each training session, going out there and doing what she could. She didn't let others intimidate her, but took on the challenge. When the program called for 10 hill repeats, she did her best to do 9 and was thrilled with doing that many.

"Doing triathlons opened up a new world for me. Now I can hold a conversation with other people who also do triathlons!" says Karen.

It's amazing how great you feel when you learn something new and take on a challenge. It's well worth stepping through the fear.

Karen completed the Park Center Tri and ran the Trek Women's Tri the following year. She's now training for the Trek Tri again, and long term wants to run a half marathon and a marathon someday.

At the group meeting before Karen's second year of training, she described her new self: a regular person who does triathlons and wants to keep doing them.

Karen:

66 I still can't believe I've done three triathlons. Each time I crossed the finish line, I was already looking forward to the next training season and the next race. After being a stay at home mom and never an athlete, training and competing were challenging new experiences for me. Meeting with the group twice a week was a great way to stay motivated. I always looked forward to the daily workouts alternating between swim, bike, and run. Three years later, I still look forward to these daily workouts and I continue to improve my endurance, distance and strength. I continue to Tri because crossing the finish line, when you never thought you could, is the greatest feeling—right up there with graduating from college, getting married, and having kids. I never could have imagined I would add the word "triathlete" to the list of other words I use to describe myself: wife, mother, friend, daughter, and sister. I look forward to every step of this journey I never thought I would be on. 99

Welcome to Training: More Than Exercise!

Now you've set your goals, acquired skill and knowledge, learned about tri gear and nutrition, and received inspiration from other women who've gone out on a limb to complete the tri journey. This is where you begin your own personal journey with the 12-week training guide. We'll show you how to follow the program week by week, giving you the knowledge and confidence to continue your journey to the finish line.

Those of you who've enjoyed exercising or training in one sport will learn to combine and train in all three sports. Cross training is far healthier and better for your body than pursuing a single sport. However, it's a learned process to focus on three sports instead of one. Even though you may be a great runner, perhaps you don't know how to swim. Or you may have to start swimming at a lower level than you're accustomed to in other sports. Don't worry; you'll increase the intensity as your fitness level allows. Cross training distributes the stress of exercise over the entire muscle network, with no single muscle group taxed beyond its limits. Cross training is the ideal way to build a solid base of aerobic fitness and full-body health.

As part of your long-term goal for completing a Sprint or Olympic distance triathlon, you'll also need to set *performance* goals. Whether you're a first timer or an experienced athlete, setting performance goals is critical to your journey. Each training phase and workout in the program is designed with the purpose of getting you over that finish line. And you will make it.

Our Sprint and Olympic distance training plans have three training phases: BASE, INTENSITY, and PEAK, each with slightly different distances and intensities, but fundamentally the same.

Base Phase: (3 weeks)

During the base phase, you focus on developing safety and fine tuning your skills in each sport. You'll start building stamina and develop overall endurance. Workouts will be low intensity, focused on form, pace, and comfort level. Adding core and strength training will help you build on your endurance as you train. This phase calls for one day of running, one day of cycling, and one day of swimming, plus at least one more day a week on your weakest sport.

Intensity Phase: (6 weeks)

The goal of this phase is to begin increasing your speed through interval training while you continue developing endurance and strength. Back to back or "brick" workouts (where you practice swim-to-bike, bike-to-run) are also introduced.

Peak Phase: (2 weeks)

During this phase, you continue building endurance and focus on getting comfortable transitioning from one sport to the next while maintaining form. You'll complete a couple of *dress rehearsal* mini-triathlons during this phase to help you know exactly what to expect on race day (more about this in a later chapter).

Taper:

One week before the race, your body must rest as the mind prepares for race day. By this time you'll be physically and mentally prepared for the race. Your body needs rest, along with passive workouts (more on this in another chapter as you reach taper week).

Start using your training schedule today: Welcome to training!

Take a moment to look at the 12 week training program in the middle of this book. This program is designed to be simple, yet cover all three phases plus the taper week. You can begin your training as you continue reading through the following chapters and gain more knowlege as you follow the program.

Your training program is organized in an easy to follow, week by week format. You can study it each week and, if you choose, look ahead to see the exciting workouts coming up. Don't worry, you'll be ready for those workouts when the time comes.

Along with a space to list a specific date 12 weeks before your race day, the plan includes a column where we list a performance goal for each session. These mini workout goals are things to keep in mind for each session. We suggest you use the journal pages to note feedback on how you felt, or whether you reached your goal for each session. Be sure to give yourself credit where credit is due as you accomplish each workout. This is highly motivating and allows you to maximize each workout, taking your training step by step in bite-size pieces.

You'll notice six workouts listed for each week. Only four workouts per week are needed to feel confident in completing the triathlon, so you have the choice of the workouts listed. If you're feeling ambitious, you may do as many as six per week, but only four are necessary. "Sometimes less is more" is a good mantra to follow, while remembering you can adjust the number of workouts per week as you gain strength. You should *always allow one day of rest per week. This is critical.*

As your training progresses each week you'll need to work your aerobic (cardiovascular) system, and your anaerobic (muscular) system. A good rule is to do one endurance building, low intensity workout a week in each sport, and only one shorter, high intensity workout per week. Hill and track workouts (speed work) should NOT be done during the same week. Never do two days in a row of intensity workouts. Follow intensity workouts with either a rest day or your long, slow, endurance workout.

The training program also includes details for each workout, incorporating time for warm-up, cool down, and stretching. Initially the workouts start at under one hour and progresses to a full two hours. Block out this time in your weekly schedule.

Note that first-time runners often go out too hard and become easily discouraged. It's important to begin with a slow shuffle. If you push your base pace and become anaerobic before you're conditioned, it takes much longer to recover, get your breath back, and start running again. This becomes a vicious, discouraging cycle, so you quit. We've heard hundreds of people say, "I just can't run, I'm not a runner." In most cases, this happens because they were starting out faster than their bodies could handle. They were essentially starting out sprinting, then would have to stop two minutes into the run. Only after you build your base should you start adding speed work. Anyone can be a runner. You just have to start with your own base instead of trying to keep up with someone who has a stronger base. For example, Karen actually jogged slowly for 30 minutes right away. She couldn't believe her accomplishment and was rewarded by learning she could run. She just needed to be a little easier on herself at the start.

COACH TIP

Training recommendations

4-day workout week = 2 days in your weakest sport plus 1 day per week in your other two strong sports.

5-day workout week = 2 days per week in your 2 weakest sports + 1 day per week in your strongest.

6-day workout week= 2 days per week, per sport.

You'll decide what works best with your lifestyle and goals. Often you may find yourself feeling energetic enough one week to fit in six workout sessions, yet the next week you can barely manage four. Don't sweat it. Listen to your body and do what feels right. Journal about what's going on in your life during these weeks—whether you're traveling, have kid's activities that take extra time, or you're feeling sick. Give yourself a break if you feel overloaded. Life gets hectic, but you can still move forward with your training.

COACH TIP

"The more you train the more recovery you need. That's when you get stronger. It takes time, so don't expect results overnight."

- Hope Martin
Together We Tri Trainer

COACH TIP

Keep your book and your training guide by your side all the time! Take it with you to work, the gym, pool, and in the car. Keep notes and journal entries as you move through each workout session. Refer back to this book often. You'll surprise yourself with your progress!

COACH TIPS

Beware of the three biggest mistakes athletes make and don't fall prey to these common blunders:

1. Working out too hard and too often. Doing so will dramatically increase the risk for physical injury and mental burnout. Plus, it doesn't allow the body to recover from the last workout, which in turn doesn't allow you to perform as well in future workouts.
2. Not going easy enough on easy days (or not taking any off days at all).
3. Always training at the same pace.

- Mary Bradbury
Together We Tri Trainer

Feeling Sick?
When to work out and when to stay in bed

If you feel a head cold coming on, it's okay to exercise. Sometimes working out will clear your sinuses and you'll feel better. If you don't feel well in your gut or gastrointestinal system, either shorten your workout, take it easy, or rest completely. Of course, if you have a fever, you should take the day off. Taxing your body when you're ill will actually lengthen your recovery time.

Soreness is normal—especially with some of the higher intensity sessions—so this isn't a reason to rest. If you're in pain, take that seriously and RICE it (as we explain in the Safety chapter)—Rest, Ice, Compress, Elevate. Do NOT keep training through pain—that will only make matters worse.

COACH TIPS

Starting your training program on your own.

- Find your pace and always work with where you are. If you can talk without panting, that's your build pace. As you grow stronger, you can push your pace in workouts to simulate race pace, but not at the beginning.
- Give yourself rewards along the way. Set up a reward system for yourself. "When I run the full three miles comfortably without stopping, I'll buy a new outfit, or upgrade my tri gear."
- Keep good technique in mind, even when you're picking up yardage. Remember efficient athletes are naturally faster athletes.

Key Points

1. Workout Phases: Base, Intensity, Peak.
2. You will taper the week before the race.
3. You'll workout either 4, 5, or 6 days a week, depending on your lifestyle.
4. Remember to train in your weakest sport most often.
5. Always allow at least one day of rest per week.
6. The training plan includes daily and weekly performance goals. Record your successes.
7. Start using your Training Plan!

NOTES

BASE TRAINING — TRIATHLON TRAINING - WEEK 1

Choose 4-6 Workouts per week. Add strength work 2-3 days a week

Date	Sport	Workout	Goal
Mon.	Run	Warm up hips, grapevine, forward and lateral leg swings, 5 minute warm up, walk or slow jog, Run 30-40m, if you are a new runner walk 2 minutes / jog 2, think of high cadence.	Welcome to training!! Review your 12-week training plan to get an idea of workouts to come. Your first few weeks, we want you to just get used to moving and introducing swim, bike, run and strength into your regular weekly routine.
Tues.	Swim or rest	5 m warm up 20-30m swim including drill work 2x50 choose 2 simple drills from your drill sheet 2x100 Rest 30 4x50s easy pace, R 30 2x50 drills, then 4x50s easy R 30.	If you are already a skilled swimmer, continue your level of training, If beginning, review how to read a swim workout, just get in the water and focus on technique. Review your drills and add to each of your swims. IF you don't finish or stick to the workouts at first. Don't worry. You have 12 weeks till race day. You will get there!
Wed.	Bike	(S) 30-45 m (O) 45-60 m Strength 10 m , 3x15 sit up sets, 3x10 push up sets.	Find your comfort zone. The first week we are getting back on the saddle and remembering what our bikes feel like. Find a nice steady cadence. EZ pace, low heart rate. Focus on technique, bike fit and high cadence (turn over) should be 80-100.
Thurs.	Rest	Remember throughout training, resting is as important as building. Continue to journal your workouts and how you feel, each week you will feel stronger!	Remember you can choose what days you do what workout. You do not have to do the planned workout on the day listed. Just make sure you do at least 4 per week, 2 of them being your weakest sport.
Fri.	Run	5 minute warm up (S) 30 m (O) 40 m, find a marked course or treadmill and try to record how long it takes you for 1 mile.	run/walkers 2 mi walk, 2mi slow jog. Remember if you have already been running more than listed, continue your current mileage if you wish for now.
Sat.	Swim	(S) 20 m, all drills, then 5 min swim cool down (O) 30 m, mainly drills. Always warm up and stretch after each work out. Strength 10 m, including squats, sit ups.	If you are already a skilled swimmer, continue your level of training. Don't over do it however, you are working on 3 separate sports. Week one is about technique, technique, technique
Sun.	Bike	Find a spin class at your club or go for a 45-60m ride, shooting for 8-12 miles YOU are on your way and off to a great start Make sure you Journal your successes	Remember your water, and of course your helmet if riding outdoors. Still concentrating on full pedal stroke, feel of your bike and fit as well as cadence, practice shifting gears to meet cadence

Workout Key: m = minutes
y = yards
mi = miles
R= rest
S=Sprint distance training workout
O=Olympic distance training workout

BASE TRAINING		TRIATHLON TRAINING - WEEK 2	
		Choose 4-6 Workouts per week. Add strength work 2-3 days a week	
Date	**Sport**	**Workout**	**Goal**
Mon.	Swim	(S) 30 m (O) 45 m Take your time, still working on technique If you don't finish the workout no worries	(A) Warm up 100 4x100 R 20, Make 2 of the 100's drills 8x50s - R 10, 4x100 - R15, Make 2 of the 100's drills 100 cool down
Tues.	Run	2-4 mile run, or run/walk Continue building endurance slowly, Follow workout with 2 sets of 15 each - sit ups, push ups and lunges	run/walkers: slowly decrease your walking time, while trying to slowly build your run time. Start very slowly. If you start sprinting you will end up anaerobic, and feeling defeated. Go SLOW
Wed.	Bike	10-15 miles, or 45-60m spin class. If you do not have a bike, you should try to secure one soon. You want to start getting saddle time on your bike in order to feel strong for race day.	2 miles warm up spinning in low gear, then practice switching gears to maintain a high cadence. If you are going up a hill and your cadence gets slower, you need to learn to switch to a higher or easier gear. And if you are going down hill and spinning out, switch to a lower or harder gear.
Thurs.	Run	(S) 2-3 miles jog, walk when needed (O) 4-5 miles Add 10 m of Core/strength work of your choice	Low intensity, remember, we are focusing on endurance right now, not speed. Keep building. Take water breaks when needed and get back to your run.
Fri.	Rest	Feel great about your baby steps and embrace your challenges. Journal something you are proud of accomplishing this week	Just a reminder to choose a minimum of 4 workouts per week and add strength work to 2-3 workouts. Always remember to stretch after each and every workout. This is imperative for injury prevention.
Sat.	Swim	100 warm up, add a new drill 1x200 followed by 100 simple drill 1x200 100 drill 1x400 100 cool down	Note that swim drills can be difficult and may tax you more than actual swimming. Please be patient. The drills will work and you will improve! If you feel your stoke is not coming along, don't be afraid to take a swim lesson or two to build your confidence
Sun.	Bike	(S)10-12 miles mod to moderate intensity, (O) 12-15 miles mod to moderate intensity, If a spin class is more convenient the first few weeks, that is fine. Around week 4 its imperative to get outdoors and gain confidence with your riding and shifting.	Continue to build endurance and get comfortable on your bike Remember how important hydrating is for all sports, **Don't forget to stretch after all workouts.**

Workout Key: m = minutes
   y = yards
   mi = miles
   R= rest
   S=Sprint distance training workout
   O=Olympic distance training workout

Date	Sport	Workout	Goal
BASE WEEK		**TRIATHLON TRAINING - WEEK 3**	
		Choose 4-6 Workouts per week. Add strength work 2-3 days a week	
Mon.	Swim	100 warm up 2x50s - R 15, 2x50 drills 2x100 - R 20, 2x50s drills 2x100 - R 20, 4x50s drills 100 = 1100	Make sure you are watching your form. When you get tired often your stroke suffers. Just stop, take a rest, and go back to basic drills. We will have plenty of time to build endurance. But its not worth building on a sloppy stroke.
Tues.	Run	(S) 20-30 m (O) 40-50 m Strength, 2x15 each, sit ups, push ups, squats, watch form.	Try to keep the pace slow enough to make it through the full run distance. If you keep your pace slow enough, you might be surprised how long you will last. Remember, while base building, no need for speed. In fact going to fast too soon is exactly what we don't want. Run slow, build slow and before long you will be running.
Wed.	Bike	(S) 12 miles or 50-60 m (O) 18 miles or 60-70 m	First 2 miles spin in a really low gear. Easy, high cadence, then ride moderate, pushing your pace slightly and cool down for your last mile. Start timing how long it takes to ride a mile.
Thurs.	Rest Tip of the week	If you are trying to lose weight, make sure you are journaling and making conscious decisions. Often you'll feel hungrier as you gain muscle and start losing weight.	Make sure you are refueling with good choices. You don't have to be perfect. But little changes make a big difference. Like getting a healthy protien carb snack within 20 minutes after your workout. This will keep you satisfied until your next meal and not famished
Fri.	Swim	(S) 35 m (O) 45 m	Warm up 200 4x100 - R 20. Make 2 100's drills 8x 50s - R 10 , 4x100, Make 2 100's drills Make sure you work on new drills, and add more skill
Sat.	Bike/Run brick	(S) 3 miles jog, walk when needed (O) 5 miles Add Core strength work of your choice	Low intensity, remember, we are focusing on endurace right now, not speed. Time your mile, and note where you have made improvements over the last few weeks. Less walking? Better endurance, greater distance? Lots of time left to build.
Sun.	Bike	(S) 12 miles mod to moderate intensity, (O) 15 miles mod to moderate intensity. You have made it through BASE training! Next week passive recovery and on with our intensity phase! You are on your way! Give yourself a pat on the back, journal and keep up the good work! Triathlete here you come!	Continue gaining comfort with your cadence and gear shifting. Practice drinking water as you ride. If you don't have a water cage on your bike, get one! The sooner you get used to hydrating on the bike, the better

Workout Key: m = minutes
y = yards
mi = miles
R= rest
S=Sprint distance training workout
O=Olympic distance training workout

RECOVERY WEEK		TRIATHLON TRAINING - WEEK 4	
		Choose 4-6 Workouts per week. Add strength work 2-3 days a week	
Date	**Sport**	**Workout**	**Goal**
Mon.	Swim	(S) 20 m EZ this is recovery week (O) 30 m EZ 100 warm up, then slow swim adding drill work	Let your body rest a little from our last 3 weeks Even when adding yardage, keep good technique in mind. If you feel your stroke is falling apart or you are tired, remember, stop and do drills.
Tues.	Bike	12-15 mile long steady ride	Moderate and steady, focus on form and race pace. Stretch! This would be a great time to practice changing a tire. Look back at the directional in this book, or go to a local bike shop for a hands on demonstration.
Wed.	Run	(S) 30 m EZ (O) 50 m EZ Add strength sets, sit ups, push ups, lunges	We will be getting more intense next week. Just continue to get your stride and slowly add to your base. Get an idea of your base mile time, so you can gauge improvements.
Thurs.	Bike	(S) 12 miles low intensity (O) 18 miles low intensity	Continue slowly building endurance. Work on RPM's. **Don't forget to stretch after all workouts.**
Fri.	Rest	Almost a quarter of the way through your training. Take time to re-assess your goals. Reward yourself for the workouts you have done.	Don't worry about the ones you have missed. Give yourself credit for your efforts and get ready for the next phase and continue learning, building and accomplishing, step, by step
Sat.	Swim	No sets today. Start with a couple drills, then a slow steady continuous swim for 20-30 minutes. See how far you can go. Strive for 400-800 yards before you rest. Record your total.	Increase yardage while maintaining technique. Will also do some open water simulation swimming. After circuits, heart rate lecture.
Sun.	Run	3-4 mile continuous run, followed by strength training	Easy run, focus on form, posture, high cadence or turn over, low intensity. We will start adding speed work soon, so take your time and enjoy your time to yourself. IF you are needing motivation its always fun to train with a group; you have a base now. Look for a local running store or church, often you can join for free and it will help you be accountable, to your weekly runs.

Workout Key: m = minutes
            y = yards
            mi = miles
            R= rest
            S=Sprint distance training workout
            O=Olympic distance training workout

INTENSITY PHASE		TRIATHLON TRAINING - WEEK 5	
		Choose 4-6 Workouts per week. Add strength work 2-3 days a week	

Date	Sport	Workout	Goal
Mon.	Run	(S) 3-4 mi or 40 m (O) 5-6 mi, or 60 m 2x15 sit ups, push ups, squats STRETCH, HYDRATE	Tempo run: short warm up then challenging pace that you can continue for full run, then cool down when you can not continue tempo pace. Also called lactate or threshold run. Try to push yourself a bit on this one. If you need to stop, get water and catch your breath, do so and come right back to finish run.
Tues.	Swim	200 warm up 2x100 drill - R 20, 4x 50s mod-fast - R 15 2x100 drill - R 20, 4X 50 speed down back easy. Followed by open water drills	After workout: Steady swim while working on OW skills. (if your race is in the open water) Otherwise add more sets in the pool. For OW, practice swimming while closing eyes, to see how straight you swim, practice navigating around kick boards in your lane (actually place in your lane) practice sighting and re-balancing.
Wed.	Bike	(S) 15 miles or 60 m (O) 20 miles or 75 m First bricks coming up. Go back and remind yourself about T1 and T2	Add 1 minute acceleration every mile. Make this ride count, practice drinking your electrolyte drink and your water. Stretch!
Thurs.	Run	(S) 3-4 miles 45-50 m (O) 5-6 miles 55-70 m Strength work, heavy on the abs this time 4 sets of 20 crunches, 2, 1-min planks	Long and easy Do some core work afterwards
Fri.	Rest	Make sure you are listening to your body and making assessments. If you are getting any aches and pains, are you stretching? Are your shoes old?	Are you pushing yourself too hard? Have you had a rough week and need some extra rest days? No workout is worth doing if rest is what you need. Make sure you journal changes, both good and bad.
Sat.	Bike	(S) 60-75 m total ride (O) 90 m total ride	Warm up 10-15 min with a few 30 second single leg spins. Then do five sets of 4 min fast intervals with at least 4 minutes EZ spin in between. Ensure to get 5-10 min EZ cool down.
Sun.	Swim	Continue adding on distance while checking form, shoot for 800-1500yds. Workout: 100 warm up, 200 kick, 200 pull, 200 triple switch, 6x50 - R15, 8x25 sprints - R15, 1x200 catch up. 100 cool down=1500,	If you have a race planned and need to practice open water, now might be a good time to look into lakes, water temperature and renting wetsuits. You will need to practice in your wetsuit at least 5-6 times prior to your race. Refer to our book for online rental suggestions if there are no local tri stores

Workout Key: m = minutes
y = yards
mi = miles
R= rest
S=Sprint distance training workout
O=Olympic distance training workout

INTENSITY PHASE		TRIATHLON TRAINING - WEEK 6		
		Choose 4-6 Workouts per week. Add strength work 2-3 days a week		
Date	**Sport**	**Workout**		**Goal**
Mon.	Run	(S) 4-5 miles (O) 6-8 miles Add strength, 2x15 sits ups, lunges, push ups.		Long easy run add several 30-60 sec pick-ups. Take at least 4 min between each acceleration. Focus on good form.
Tues.	First T2 Brick Bike/run	(S) 12 miles/10 min run (O) 18 miles/15 min run Remember, this will not feel natural going from bike to run. Take your time.		Bring gear for both sports, take your time during your transition, change to your run gear, drink some water, and start your run. Start with a really slow shuffle for the first couple minutes. Don't worry if your legs feel like lead. That will change with practice
Wed.	Swim	(S) continue adding on distance checking form, shoot for 800-1200 yards (O) shoot for 1500-2000 yards		Long Distance swim, take breaks when needed. Moderate pace. Remember to always follow an interval workout or really intense workout with a rest day or passive distance day. Never do back-to-back intensity days
Thurs.	Bike	(S)15-20 miles (O)25-30 miles		Long Distance ride. Moderate pace. Take stretch breaks if needed. Just get in the distance. Practice cadence and drinking on the bike.
Fri.	Rest	As you are building your distance and intensity. Listen to your body, Try not todo back-to-back sports. Max distances for Sprint are swim is 1200 yards		Bike 18 miles, Run 5 miles. There is no need to go beyond these max distances unless you are ready for the challenge. OLY: Swim: 2400 yards, Bike,36mi, Run:9
Sat.	Run Hill Repeats	Warm up run 5 min, then do 6-10 hill repeats do 10 push ups and 10 lunges after each hill. then back up the hill. Remember to hydrate		This will be an intense workout. This workout will definitely take you beyond your anaerobic or lactatete threshold level. You will be out of breath, recover and go again. This intense interval work will make your easy pace runs faster with less effort than before.
Sun.	Swim	(S) 1000-1200 yards (O) 2000-2200 yards		Mix endurance and drills. End with 4-6 25's sprint, 20 seconds rest in between. Finish with drills

Workout Key: m = minutes
                 y = yards
                 mi = miles
                 R= rest
                 S=Sprint distance training workout
                 O=Olympic distance training workout

INTENSITY PHASE		TRIATHLON TRAINING - WEEK 7	
		Choose 4-6 Workouts per week. Add strength work 2-3 days a week	
Date	**Sport**	**Workout**	**Goal**
Mon.	Run	(S) 4-6 miles (O) 7-9 miles	Low-mod intensity, still working on slowly building your mileage to your max levels needed. Don't forget about form, posture, cadence, hydration. Add a few slight 20 sec accelerations 1-2 per mile, then recover.
Tues.	First T1 Brick Swim/Bike	(S) Swim-800 yards, Bike-8 miles (O)Swim 1600yards, Bike- 15 miles, Brick can be done in the pool or open water. You might feel a little dizzy when you first get out of the water. That will change as you practice.	Bring your equipment for both the swim and bike. Take your time transitioning from sport to sport. You will feel soggy and wet as you start your bike. Start in a low gear where you can easily spin, then add more resistance, continue your 80-100 cadence
Wed.	Run	(S) 10 min w-up, 4x800's sprint, 2 min rest (O) 20 min w-up, 4x1600's sprint, 4 min rest Then 5 min cool down, can be done on a quarter mile track or find a marked mile.	Speed work followed by core. Really try to push your pace. Its not very comfortable, but will help you become a faster stronger runner. This work out is intense, but short. Yesterday was long, but not intense, so these are complimentary workouts
Thurs.	Swim	(S) 20 min or 1/2 mi open water (O)30 min or 1-1.5 mi open water, if possible, Continue to practice sighting drills.	This workout should be easy with some drills. Continue working on reaching your max distance. IF you have a lake race, you should try to do most of your swims now in open water.
Fri.	Rest	STAY MOTIVATED!!! You are doing great! Journal your successes. You have made it thru the 2nd phase of training. Feel proud of how far you have come.	We often notice motivation waning a little around a month out from the race, fears try to creep in to convince you, you won't be ready. YOU WILL BE READY!! Come up with Mantras to help.
Sat.	Brick Bike - Run repeats	Find a mile loop or 2 mile in and out (S) 4 laps bike, 2 laps run repeat x3 (O) 4 laps bike, 2 laps run repeat x5 So 4 mile bike and 2 mile run repeats.	Bring all bike and run gear, as well as hydration and a good attitude! This one is challenging, but fun to practice T2 multiple times. Do these with mod intensity, get thru all of the repeats.
Sun.	Swim	(S) 1 mile open water or pool (O) 1.5 mile open water or pool	Start with a few drills, Strong continuous swim, do some pick-ups. To accelerate your pace start trying on wet suits if you have not yet, and also think through your gear. What works? What needs to be changed.

Workout Key: m = minutes
          y = yards
          mi = miles
          R= rest
          S=Sprint distance training workout
          O=Olympic distance training workout

Date	Sport	Workout	Goal
		RECOVERY WEEK TRIATHLON TRAINING - WEEK 8 *Choose 4-6 Workouts per week. Add strength work 2-3 days a week*	
Mon.	Run	(S) 2-3 miles (O) 3 -4miles Strength work 2x15, sit ups, push ups, lunges	EZ- this is a recovery week, but you can add a couple 20 second accelerations. It is important to give yourself this week, in order to be rested for your final phase of training.
Tues.	Swim	EZ Swim, really focus on technique this week. Do 2-3 sets of drills, Then (S)-20 min swim, (O)-30min	Chance to increase comfort in the lake, practice spotting and coming up with your mantras and rescue stroke should you get nervous in the water.
Wed.	Bike	(S) 12 miles (O) 20 miles	EZ ride - this is a recovery week. Keep cadence high (88-100) and keep heart rate low.
Thurs.	Your choice	Good chance to work on your weakest sport... Hint, hint.	Duration can be moderately long, but intensity low-mod. Enjoy your workout, feel your evolving confidence and strength
Fri.	Rest	Now is a good time to go back to day one and read your reasons for starting this goal. You have come so far, give yourself a pat on the back	the credit you deserve for sticking to it. So what if you have missed a few key workouts here or there, you are on your way to becoming a Triathlete. Keep it up!
Sat.	Bike-run brick	(S) 6 mile bike & 2 mile run. (O) 10 mile bike & 4 mile run.	EZ intensity. Bring hydration & all run/cycling gear. This is a good chance to test whatever fuel you'd like.
Sun.	Swim	(S) 800 yds (O) 1600 yds 1/2mi - 1mi open water Strength: sit ups, push ups, squats.	EZ swim, do lots of drills. Ensure you are rotating and finishing your stroke. Nice and smooth!

Workout Key: m = minutes
y = yards
mi = miles
R= rest
S=Sprint distance training workout
O=Olympic distance training workout

PEAK TRAINING   TRIATHLON TRAINING - WEEK 9

Choose 4-6 Workouts per week. Add strength work 2-3 days a week

Date	Sport	Workout	Goal
Mon.	Run	(S) 4-5mi (O) 6-8mi Start slow for first 10, then speed up to Tempo run for 20-30m, strength and cool down.	Tempo run is just shy of your race pace. If your slow endurance days are 12 minute miles, and your fast mile is 10 min miles. make 20-30 minutes somewhere in between that pace. You should be pushing yourself, but not an all out. Stretch refuel.
Tues.	T1 Swim/Bike Brick	Lay out all needed for T1 transition, practice transition as if real race. Try to improve T1 (S) Swim-800 yards, Bike-10 Moderate pace (O) Swim-1600yards, Bike-18, Moderate pace.	Don't forget hydration and fuel and all equipment needed. This is a great opportunity to work on transitions. Peak phase is all about working out the kinks and perfecting transitioning from sport to sport
Wed.	Swim	(S) 1000 yds slow steady (O) 2000 yds slow steady Practice using glide with your wet suit. Start choosing race day base layer, find fav tri suit.	If you feel you need to work technique, do lots of drills. If not, get in a good workout focusing on maintaining good form.
Thurs.	Brick Bike/Run	(S) 10 mi Ride/2mi Run (O) 20 mi Ride/3mi Run Strength, Ab focus, Planks, sit-ups, bicycle sets	Gear check, have you practiced changing a tire? Do you intend to change your tires to slicks? Are you due for a new pair of running shoes? Now is the time to do a gear check and practice in your race day choices in a short few weeks.
Fri.	Rest	Start visualizing yourself crossing the finish line as you continue to build strength, speed and perfect your transitions. Don't let self-doubt creep in. Journal where you see yourself	Start seeing yourself with the joy of success as you cross that finish line Journal all of your fears and current and future rewards. You are getting close to your goals!
Sat.	Bike	Long slow-moderate ride with accelerations. (S) 18-25 miles, (O) 30-35 miles Every few miles, add 1-min speed intervals.	Feel free to do a very short 5 min run afterwards, just to feel that transition demand, but do not do any distance. Take a break if needed, after a long ride like this, your race distance feels like a breeze.
Sun.	Swim	Drills, speed (S) 800 yards (O) 1600 yards Strength, 2x15 push ups, sit ups, squats.	100 warm up, 2x 100 drills of choice. 10x50s Speed down recover back R 30 cool down.

Workout Key: m = minutes
               y = yards
               mi = miles
               R= rest
               S=Sprint distance training workout
               O=Olympic distance training workout

PEAK PHASE		**Triathlon Training - Week 10**	
		Choose 4-6 Workouts per week. Add strength work 2-3 days a week	
Date	**Sport**	**Workout**	**Goal**
Mon.	Run	(S) 30 min (O) 45 min Strength: sit-ups, push ups, lunges, dips	Warm-up and do drills 10-15 minutes. Find a flat grassy area and run 20-30 second accelerations emphasizing quick and proud posture. Take 2 minutes in between with jogging or walking for total of 30-45. 5 min cool down
Tues.	Brick Bike - run repeats	Find a mile loop or 1 mile out and back (S) 2 laps bike, 1 laps run repeat x5 (O) 2 laps bike, 1 laps run repeat x 7-8 So 4 mile bike and 2 mile run repeats	Set up your T2 as you would for race day, bring what you will wear for race day, your fuel, gels, shots, whatever you will use. Workout should be done with Moderate intensity. Try to simulate your transition from sport to sport, going directly from one to the other. Transitions are always hard, but they should seem easier than that first one a month ago
Wed.	Swim	(S) 3/4-1 mi open water, (O)1.5 open water, Remember there is never a need to go over your max distances needed to be race ready. But if you feel strong and want a little buffer, you can go over those distances slightly.	Swim continuous - no stopping and add 5-10 30-40 second bursts. Really work on keeping a long smooth stroke and don't forget to sight. Visualize yourself in that swim, going through the race and having a smooth strong swim.
Thurs.	Bike	(S) 15-20 mi (O)20-30mi Warm-up in an easy gear, then do one 20 minute interval at race pace. Recover at least 5 minutes then the remainder of the ride, sprinkle in a few 10 second sprints.	Do a 5-10 minute EZ run right after you get off your bike. These are your last few bricks to work on any part of your race/training that you need to.
Fri.	Rest	You are a couple weeks away from race day. Take a moment to read your goals again and realize how far you have come.	Do whatever is needed to be prepared about your expectations: your best case scenario as well as any fears. Work through them with, realistic solutions and goals. See yourself feeling strong on your entire race. Journal how you think you will feel.
Sat.	Mini-Tri	Dress Rehearsal. Putting it ALL together! (S) Swim - 1/2mi, Bike - 10mi, Run - 2mi (O) Swim-1mi, Bike-18mi, Run-3mi . Make sure you have a plan, map out your exact routes, where you will place your gear, where you will swim, bike and run, Know your turn around points.	Focus on your transitions, remember to stay hydrated and fueled. Practice in your racing gear to make sure it fits and feels right. Again, note what you eat beforehand. The first time you put it all together, you will be apprehensive. And it is tiring. But you will prove to yourself that you can do it. Journal what worked, what needs to change for next one.
Sun.	Run	(S) 5 miles (O) 8 miles Strength: sit-ups, push ups, lunges, dips.	EZ pace, Enjoy your slow steady run. This is your last mileage run before your race, We will take it a little easier the next week, preparing for our race and taper.

Workout Key: m = minutes
  y = yards
  mi = miles
  R= rest

PEAK PHASE		**Triathlon Training - Week 11, Passive Recovery**	
		Choose 4-6 Workouts per week. Add strength work 2-3 days a week	
Date	**Sport**	**Workout**	**Goal**
Mon.	Swim	(S) 3/4-1 mi open water (O) 1.5 open water If your race is open water, make sure you have practiced in your wet suit	Swim EZ, keep your form, don't sacrifice good technique for speed. Include some drills and 5-6 30 second bursts. Remember this is your peak phase and last week prior to taper. Make this week count. Start reviewing race course and checking current water temps.
Tues.	Brick Swim/Bike	(S) Swim 1/2 mi, Bike 15 mi (O) Swim 1 mi, Bike-18 mi Think about your stroke and technique. Start all swims with a slow catch up drill to calm your nerves. Practice sighting and have mantras ready if you get nervous.	Have a transition set up. Ensure to have anything you would use during a race; hydration, gels, Body Glide/Suit Juice, helmet, glasses. Also, remember what you eat before this workout and see if your tummy is ok with it during and afterwards. Know your plan.
Wed.	Bike	Do 4x6 minute intervals at max intensity with a 4 min recovery in between. Cool down at least 15 minutes. Remember cadence and gears, Also hydration.	Short, but intense. This will remind you of what it feels like come race day and your heart rate is elevated. Practice recovering.
Thurs.	Rest	Start thinking of your race day plan, who to drive down with, your estimated time, for each event, Journal your hopes and how you feel on your last week of training prior to taper week and race day!	Check all your gear for each discipline and ensure all is in good condition. Lube your bike if need be, check brakes and wear on tires, the week prior to taper is a good time to get a tune up, if you feel its needed. Don't wait until the day before your race. You will want to test drive and make sure all is in working order
Fri.	Run	(S) 40 min (O) 60 min Strength, 2x15 push ups, squats, 2-1 min planks.	EZ pace with 5-7 30 second accelerations Enjoy this run and feel your strength. Trust in your training. And look forward to your reward.
Sat.	Mini -Tri	Last dress rehearsal before race day. (S) Swim- .5 mi, Bike- 8 mi, Run- 2 mi (O) Swim- 1 mi, Bike- 15 mi, Run-3 mi	This is a final low intensity dress rehearsal. You should be feeling race ready. You have gone through a thorough routine and dress rehearsals. Use this final min-tri to make sure everything is in order and all gear is race ready. And your plan is solid
Sun.	Choice	Swim - (S) 1/2 mi, (O)1 mi open water Bike - (S) 10-12 mi, (O) 18-22 mi Run -(S) 2 mi, (O) 5 mi	Pick your workout today—whatever feels right. Nice comfortable pace today. No intensity. Its time to start giving your body a rest, prepare mentally and emotionally. You are ready physically!

Workout Key: m = minutes
y = yards
mi = miles
R= rest
S=Sprint distance training workout
O=Olympic distance training workout

RACE WEEK - TAPER	**Triathlon Training - Week 12**		

Choose one swim, one bike, one run, and one short brick of choice

Date	Sport	Workout	Goal
Mon.	Swim	(S) Swim - 600 y (O) Swim-1200 y	Do a little speed work, but maintain form. If your race is local, do these passive workouts on the course. If not, look on the site and get a feel for the course with the maps. Read about check in and packet pick up details. Know the rules!
Tues.	Run	(S) 20 m (O) 30 m Add a few 15 second accelerations	Again easy pace, Enjoy your slow passive run as you recover and prepare for your big day. Observe how strong you feel, and how far you have come. In a few days, you will be a Triathlete! Journal your estimated race times and where your family can find you on race day.
Wed.	Bike	(S) 40 min (O) 60 min EZ ride with a few accelerations	Remember high cadence and gear shifting. Do not push this ride at all, just add a few accelerations to make sure shifting is all in order. If at all possible ride a bit on your actual race bike course. You should be getting excited, you are nearing the finish line! Journal how much this accomplishment means too you now, after all of your hard work.
Thurs.	Swim / Bike or Bike / run	(S) Swim: 10 min/20min bike, (O) Swim: 15min/30min bike (S) 20 min bike/5min run (O) 30 min bike/10 run CHOOSE ONLY 1 BRICK!!	EZ. You are going thru the motions, visualizing your smooth transition from sport to sport. You have done the work, you have put in the time. Enjoy your last workout and visualize yourself with all of the joy you will feel as you succeed, Sunday!
Fri.	Rest EXPO Check-in	No workout today. You'll feel tempted to do more this week than scheduled. Don't do it! This is your time to rest and gain strength for race day. Sit back relax eat well, get a good nights sleep, tonight's rest is imperative. Typically you don't sleep great the night before the race.	Check-in at EXPO, pick up your packet, write down your race number and wave, double check that you have your chip, cap and stickers for bike, helmet and race belt. Check your gear list and lay everything out. Make sure nothing is missing. You'll be feeling nervous. But rest assured you are ready.
Sat. Group	Rest Expo Check -in	Rest again today. Usually you can check in Fri. or Sat. Try to stay off your feet and take it easy, eat well, hydrate well. Place your stickers on your gear, go thru your check list one more time and then pack your gear bag for the morning. Journal your excitement for your reward!	You can get body marked at the Expo or race day morning. Make sure you take the time to go to the transition area and do a walk thru. It will relieve race morning anxiety if you have a visual of the area. Get some rest! As you go to sleep do a final visualization of your entire race and how well your day will go!
Sun. Race Day!	RACE	Stay focused - you can do it!!! Race with confidence and pride for all that you have put into this day. Enjoy your moment!	FINISH LINE! Congratulations! YOU ARE NOW A TRIATHLETE!!

Workout Key: m = minutes
y = yards
mi = miles

Congratulations!

Enjoy your new accomplishment. Share your success and inspire others to *TRI THE JOURNEY*! Remember to record your finish line experience, so you can look back and remember how great it feels to follow through with your plan and accomplish your dreams!

NOTES

CHAPTER 7

Build Your Endurance and Speed

> *"Obstacles are those frightful things you see
> when you take your eyes off your goals."*
> - Unknown.

WITHIN MINUTES, KATHY RYAN'S life took a brutal, and unexpected twist. During the delivery of her twin girls, she was whisked into surgery for a cesarean section—and that's when things went strangely awry.

Kathy Ryan

While in the recovery room, she went into shock and was rushed back into the operating room where doctors discovered her uterine artery had been cut during the c-section, and she was bleeding internally. The surgeons found the cut artery and repaired it, but she still required about 30 blood transfusions and was put on life support. After a few unstable days, she came to, but then had difficulty with blood clots, which unfortunately led to a pulmonary embolism (a blood clot traveled to her lung) and required a chest tube for about a week. She wasn't nearly out of the woods. More setbacks occurred.

While in the hospital she faced multiple infections and Methicilloin-resistant Staphylococcus Aureus (MRSA), a bacterial infection resistant to common antibiotics. Kathy battled for two months just to stay alive. When she was finally cleared to go home, walking up and down the stairs and caring for her babies was a daily challenge.

"After I came home from the hospital, I remember looking into the mirror and didn't recognize myself. I was staring at a sickly, dying person," says Kathy, mom of three and a special education teacher.

Kathy Ryan

Before she became a wife, mother, and teacher, Kathy was on the swim and basketball teams in high school, so seeing herself out of shape and declining in health was difficult. She vowed to become healthy again.

When she was ready and her doctors gave the go-ahead, three months after giving birth to her twins, Kathy and her husband, Kevin, went to the local indoor track. She could barely make it around the track one time without pain and dizziness. Scar tissue in her lungs caused (and still causes) reoccurring pain, which worsens when she breathes deeply, coughs, or sneezes. She was shocked. In her mind she was healthy, but her body was far from it.

Six years after her near death experience, Kathy was inspired by Libby, her neighbor, to do a triathlon. With Libby's encouragement and the support of her husband and kids, Kathy decided it was time to take the tri journey, get back in shape, and finish a triathlon.

"When I first started training I had aches and pains right away. I pulled a muscle in my leg since I hadn't run for so long. But as I trained, I felt myself get stronger and stronger. I went from barely being able to run, to running a half a mile without stopping, and then was able to finish the whole tri without stopping," says Kathy.

Her schedule was hectic—a husband, three kids, and a job—fitting in workouts was a challenge. She admits she was exhausted at the end of the day and some evenings didn't feel like cycling 15 miles, but once she started, she felt exhilarated. Kathy found great joy working out with buddies—other women she bonded with who helped keep her motivated.

She finished an all women's Trek triathlon after completing the 12 week training program in this book. Kathy crossed that finish line with a feeling of "Oh, my gosh, I did it!" She, and her family were beyond proud. During this process, Kathy got fit, completed her goal of finishing the tri, and felt fulfilled emotionally, something she hadn't experienced for a long time.

"I finally felt I was myself again. I was back to the old me! I'd become healthy again and my body was back. Now I have energy to spare and my children see me fulfilled with an activity outside of family and work," explains Kathy, who went on to complete the Trek tri the following year. Her goal was to build endurance and speed—and she did.

Kathy overcame so much and inspired many others to face their fear and physical hurdles to arrive at a happier, healthier place.

Kathy:

66For quite a while, I lacked energy, strength, and self-confidence. Training for and completing a triathlon changed my life in many ways. Not only have I met many amazing people during this journey, I also started to believe in myself again. At first I was fighting to get better for my family. Over time, I realized I needed to do this for myself—to feel whole again. Several times along the way (including when I was sick) I felt like giving up. I am so proud of myself for persevering and fighting to become strong. I feel blessed to have this chance.99

You've Got Power: Intensity and Speed Training

Once you've built stamina by following the Base Phase for three weeks—improving your technique and endurance with low intensity workouts—you'll be ready to move into the Intensity Phase for the next six weeks.

With this structured exercise regime, the training plan is designed specifically to incorporate an intensity phase and build on top of each previous phase. Don't be intimidated. Move from one work out to the next for the sheer enjoyment of exercising, and you'll gradually find increased speed and muscular endurance.

The goal of the intensity phase is to further refine and enhance the systems your body needs for your targeted race. While continuing to build aerobic endurance, you will also focus on anaerobic endurance and power. Yes, power! This training phase is important for you to endure a long race, beyond one hour, with power—so you don't fatigue too quickly and can make it through your entire race feeling strong and prepared.

You'll see in the schedule that interval and speed training are introduced during this phase.

Benefits to intensity training

Intensity training increases your speed and muscular endurance, which enables you to exercise at a higher intensity without reaching exhaustion. As you stress your body with the right challenging workouts, then let yourself recover, your body will adapt and your fitness level will transform. When competing in a Sprint triathlon, you'll probably be on the course for over an hour (perhaps two hours for first timers), and then two and a half to three or more hours on an Olympic distance, so you need to prepare your body to work hard for long periods of time and still have energy.

Training at your Anaerobic Threshold (also known as Lactate Threshold), can increase your body's ability to resist fatigue and pain, and condition your body to work longer before exhaustion.

As you follow the training guide and complete intense speed workouts, you'll gain power. Intensity workouts for each sport—swim/bike/run—are built into the program. You'll notice you never actually do the full length "race" distance until the day of your actual race, but your body will be prepared. Our rules for max training distances for each sport ensure you'll be able to complete your race distance. You'll train distance and a half for each sport. So build to 3/4-mile-swim max, 5-mile-run max, and 18-mile-bike max (which is distance and half of each leg for the sprint distance race). If you've already been training in one of these sports and are starting at a higher base, feel free to go a little above these distances if you want a challenge. Be sure you don't violate the 10-15% increase rule. The distances listed are more than adequate for you to feel fully prepared.

Types of Intensity/Speed Workouts

Intervals: alternating between fast and slow. Work/Rest intervals can be a variety of lengths, depending upon your goal.

For example, after a 15 minute warm up, run five to eight, 30 second accelerations, leaving at least three minutes of easier running between each one. Leave 10 minutes for easy cool down at the end.

Or when cycling, after a 15 to 20 minute warm up, cycle hard for five minutes, then five minute easy, alternating during a 20 to 30 minute session, leaving 10 minutes to ride easy for a cool down.

Fartleks: comes from the Swedish word for "speed play." A fartlek is unstructured interval training; random accelerations with a duration and speed of your choice. These are intended to push your pace during a workout. Fartleks are considered speed work. For example, run 4 miles, add 8 fartleks—2 per mile. Sprint from one tree or light post to the next, 20, 30, and 40 yards away. While cycling, maintain 80-100 rpms, while adding in fartleks, practice shifting to maintain cadence.

A reminder to you run/walkers: if you're still building during your intensity phase, you can still do interval and speed work, then recover with a walk if need be. It's important to start building on your intensity even if you are not "running" the entire workout.

Hill Repeats: repeated hill climbs done at a fast pace with a recovery between each climb. For example, run five to eight repeats up a hill and downhill to cool down.

When incorporating higher intensity workouts into your schedule it's important to follow the "hard-easy" principle. Hard workouts should be followed by easy workouts the following day to help your body recover. During recovery, which consists of a workout with little to no intensity and a decrease in the length of exercise, your body repairs itself and grows stronger. During recovery periods, the tears in tendons and ligaments you created from intense workouts have time to repair. When this happens, you gain strength and can better tackle upcoming workloads. This is when you'll notice improvements in your ability to do workouts at a higher intensity and see your speed and endurance improving.

COACH TIP

"Start with short durations of intensity in each sport and build on length."

-Hope Martin
Together We Tri Trainer

COACH TIP
Hill training benefits
Hill training...
- helps develop power and muscle elasticity,
- improves stride frequency and length,
- develops coordination, encouraging the proper use of arm action during the driving phase and feet in the support phase,
- develops control and stabilization as well as improved speed (downhill running),
- promotes strength endurance,

- develops maximum speed and strength (short hills), and
- improves lactate tolerance (mixed hills).

COACH TIP

"When training 'long hills' most of your energy comes from aerobic sources, but steep hill climbs allow for accumulation of blood lactate and usually are anaerobic. Your leg muscles will tire, and possibly the abdominal muscles, but what causes you to bonk and tire is when you reach the limits of your cardio abilities and current trained capacity. That's when you begin to improve, with continued interval anaerobic work."

-Matt Dublin,
Together We Tri Trainer

COACH TIPS

Matt's hill climbing cycling tips:

1. Pick up your speed and a high cadence to build momentum as you approach the hill.

2. When you get to the bottom of the hill and begin climbing, shift to an easier gear when needed, but concentrate on maintaining your momentum and spinning a high cadence (near 100 rpm).

3. Shift as needed to pedal a high cadence smoothly while remaining seated, without bouncing or rocking. This is commonly known as ratcheting your gears.

4. At the top, if you need to stand up, do so, but continue to pedal a high cadence.

5. Don't stop right at the top of the hill. Instead, continue your effort until you regain speed on the descent.

6. Repeat.

-Matt Dublin
Together We Tri Trainer

COACH TIP

"Being sore is simply your body adjusting to a new activity, a new level of intensity, a longer workout, hill work etc. I'm not talking about pain here. With real pain, you need to stop. With soreness, keep going. Stretching, ice and ibuprofen can help."

-Mary Bradbury
Together We Tri Trainer

Three Basic Energy Systems

Your body uses a combination of three systems during workouts and as a triathlete. We are primarily concerned with developing our body's *aerobic metabolism,* which occurs when the body uses oxygen to create energy. This is an efficient way for the body to exercise for long periods of time.

The aerobic zone is our base building zone. Staying in your aerobic zone is actually one of your most efficient fat burning phases, but you don't get much muscle break down, hence little muscle repair or building. You will slowly build endurance by staying in this zone, but you'll never improve your speed or become a faster athlete if you don't move out of your aerobic zone.

1. *Creatine: Phosphate system* - the system that provides energy for muscular contraction in periods no longer than 5 to 10 seconds.

2. *Glycolysis* - production of energy by the breakdown of glucose or glycogen (stored sugar). Lactic acid is a by-product of this energy system (energy lasts up to two minutes).

3. *Aerobic Metabolism* - production of adenosine triphosphate (ATP or energy) through the body's use of oxygen.

Monitoring Intensity

So, how do you know when you're working hard enough to improve your fitness level to complete a triathlon? Self-monitoring your intensity by observing your exercise level will help you ensure you're working out hard enough, and relaxing the pace sufficiently on easy days to reap the benefits.

One way to gauge how hard you're working is by measuring your heart rate (HR). You'll find a wide range between resting heart rate and your maximum heart rate during a tough workout. A simple calculation will help you to know how high your heart rate should go:

Target heart rate formula

220 minus age = predicated max heart rate/beats per minute

Max HR x exercise intensity (%) = Training Zone

For example, a 40 year old female triathlete has a predicated Max Heart Rate of 180 beats per minute. Her Threshold Intensity Zone is

180 x 85% = 153 beats per minute

180 x 95% = 171 beats per minute

Her heart rate should be between 153 — 171 beats per minute while she's exercising at high intensity—doing intervals such as running, cycling, or swimming accelerations for 20 to 30 seconds.

When exercising to your max, take a moment to find your pulse at the side of your neck or your wrist and count your heartbeat for 6 seconds. Then add a zero to find your beats per minute.

You can also gauge your intensity by using the Rate of Perceived Exertion (RPE), which is a basic zero to ten scale. Zero represents a resting state, while ten is working out on the maximum level you can achieve without falling down unconscious. RPE will be different for everyone and is a reliable measure of your heart rate without worrying about fancy calculations.

Heart Rate Training Intensity Zones

Intensity level percentages will differ slightly depending on how you gauge intensity.

Recovery - Zone 1: Consists of easy workouts and interval workouts for the purpose of rejuvenating the body. Intensity is low (less than 60% of max HR).

Endurance - Zone 2: In this zone, intensity is used for long endurance workouts from 30 minutes to three hours. You should be able to carry on a conversation comfortably while exercising at this level. Here you'll build aerobic capacity working at 60% to 85% of your Max Heart Rate.

Threshold - Zone 3: Here you'll be exercising at a moderate to high intensity level while on the edge—slightly below or just above the lactate/anaerobic threshold—lasting 20 to 60 minutes. Workouts are maximally aerobic and a significant portion is done anaerobically. Zone 3 is critical for triathletes because it improves lactate tolerance and removal. Training in Zone 3 is where you'll really start to notice strength and endurance changes. You'll be working out at 85% to 95% of your Max Heart Rate.

Anaerobic endurance/power - Zone 4: Consists of high intensity training lasting 15 seconds to three minutes. Intervals, or periods of acceleration and then rest/recovery, are used in this zone to stimulate fast-twitch muscle fibers and improve lactate tolerance and clearance. Your body learns to efficiently remove lactic acid built up in the muscles. Be careful not to do too much too often at this level, because it can lead to over training. Work at this level with caution and follow it with long recovery periods. You'll be exercising at 95% plus of Max Heart Rate).

COACH TIP

Periodization happens when base training at low intensity supports later, higher intensity workouts. The right combination of exercise, rest, intensities, in the right sequence (given in your training plan) should lead to optimal performances.

Key Points

1. During the intensity phase you will refine and enhance the specific systems your body needs for your targeted race.

2. Training at your Anaerobic Threshold/Lactate Threshold can increase your body's ability to resist fatigue and pain, and condition the body to work longer before exhaustion.

3. Intensity workouts include: Intervals, fartleks, and hill repeats.

4. Remember recovery and rest are important parts of your training to help your body prepare for an endurance event.

5. Monitor your intensity by finding your target heart rate and knowing your training intensity zones.

NOTES

CHAPTER 8

Start Brick Workouts

"There are no shortcuts in life's greatest achievements."

-Anonymous

IN THE SPRING OF 2001, Jamie Damato Migdal had enough of carrying 190 pounds on her five feet four inch body frame. She was tired of wearing size 14 clothes that were tight on her. She wanted to change her life, but as a pack-a-day smoker for 15 years who couldn't swim, had never run, and didn't own a bike, the idea of getting into a fitness program seemed overwhelming.

Jamie Damato Migdal

To figure it all out and get into shape, Jamie joined Chicago's Lakeshore Athletic Club, where she noticed a Together We Tri information poster. Despite not knowing anything about it, she jumped right in, signed up, and started training for a triathlon.

Jamie had never swum a stroke in her life when she entered the club's indoor pool for her first triathlon swim session. She gave the drills her best effort, but needed to start with something even more basic. During her first swim, she and Libby focused on floating and balance concepts, plus feeling comfortable with her head and face in the water. They began blowing bubbles and by the end of session one, Jamie was starting to perfect her forward and bilateral side balance—essential for building on your stroke.

Jamie remembers: "Libby stood on the platform and told me, 'You have awesome body awareness, Jamie. You have a good mind/body connection. With a little effort and focus, before long you'll be a confident swimmer.' Her compliment was so profound for me, it influenced the rest of my life. I think of that comment all the time."

Jamie Damato Migdal

The owner of a dog training business, Jamie's background didn't include a single sport, much less three of them. She cared more about living healthier with a new set of skills than accomplishing a personal best. And the "doing" wasn't easy—she was intimidated by everything; the gear, bricks, racing. Putting it all together seemed massive.

But working through the intimidation and fears was worthwhile. As Jamie progressed to the second phase of training, bricks were added to the workouts. She heard from others in the group that brick training was difficult at first and she might feel discouraged after her first brick experience, but Jamie kept thinking positive thoughts during her first bike-to-run workout. She cycled for about 30 minutes, and then did a short ten minute run. She was only six weeks into the program and still felt a bit out of shape, but managed to complete this first brick.

Jamie explains, "I always looked forward to my workouts and never felt overwhelmed by bricks. I loved doing the swim-to-bike brick. As

I became a better swimmer, I loved feeling great when finishing the swim, drying off with my towel, wiping my feet, and feeling refreshed and wet when getting on the bike and heading out to cycle."

Many moments on her journey were fun and life changing. She recalls the specific time during a brick training run, near the end of mile three (working at her usual 10- minute mile pace), when she saw the coaches in the distance and felt total euphoria. She was breathing easily and felt like she was running on a cloud. Her running was beyond effortless. *Oh my God! she told herself, I just had my first runner's high and it felt great! I'm finally a runner.*

A Life Changing Summer

During that life-changing summer Jamie lost 50 pounds and completed the first of many triathlons. Ironically, she kept smoking during training, despite trying to quit. As her training and respect for herself developed, and she became a stronger athlete, Jamie finally quit for good in 2005. She admits that smoking hindered her training goals and slowed her progress.

Jamie has kept her weight down and says she loves her "new" body and the discipline involved with training for a triathlon. Triathlon has helped her become a better business person by making her more accountable and productive. She developed a strong belief in herself and is more likely to stand up for what she believes in. She even met her husband through triathlon training.

Jamie's triathlon experiences with fellow women led to deep friendships. She met Stefanie Levi through mutual friends, and then they trained together. In the 2002 Water's Edge tri in Naperville, Illinois, Stef was riding her new bike when she suddenly couldn't shift gears. Jamie waited for her in T2, beginning to worry as time passed. Stef finally arrived walking next to her bike into T2, crying. Jamie told her not to worry, they would finish together. They exited T2, and did a run-walk together, as Stef was still teary, unable to focus. They crossed the finish line hand in hand. Both women realized that the race isn't about ending time—it's about the shared experiences. During seven triathlons, Jamie and Stef have always watched out for each other's best interests and encouraged one another along the way.

In another tri race, Jamie swam against white-caps in the water. As she struggled with high winds and the slap of waves, Stef, who was also in the race, swam beside her until she knew Jamie was safe. Finally, Jamie felt the turbulent water was more than she could handle and decided to signal for help. The lifeguards pulled her to safety. Although she was officially disqualified from the race, she decided to run into transition, ride the bike course, and then continued into T2 to get her shoes to finish the run course. She crossed the finish line feeling accomplished despite her rough start.

Jamie has now completed 15 to 20 triathlons in eight years, including Half Ironmans. She endured a few injuries, including a blown out shoulder while lifting heavy weights without a spotter, but rehabilitated herself with rest and an appropriate training regime. She has also coached for two summers.

Jamie:

❝I love and admire the sport. Triathlon created a whole new community for me, beyond what words can say. Whenever I'm having any kind of self-doubt, I think about triathlon. I feel I can overcome anything. I truly use this experience and what it's done for me.❞

It's a Brick Workout: Build Your Bricks

Doing back-to-back workouts in two different sports doesn't come naturally to most people. Don't be surprised if this feels awkward at first, but you'll adjust with practice. The combination of three sports—swim, bike, and run—are what differentiates the triathlon from the single sport events and frankly, makes training a bit more interesting since you need to practice combining two, then eventually all three sports in one training session.

A *brick* workout means combining two of the sports back-to-back—such as a bike workout followed by a run, OR a run followed by a cycling workout, OR a swim then cycle, OR swim then run workout. The term *brick* originally referred to the cycle-to-run workout, because the athlete's legs literally feel like bricks after doing two sports. Bricks are an imperative step to build your stamina and train your body for the multisport race.

With cycling, you use more of your quadriceps (the thigh muscles) for pedaling, while running uses more of your hamstrings (behind your thighs) to propel you forward. When you stop cycling and begin to run, you'll need a few minutes to get your running legs oriented (and your mind, too). Your legs will feel heavy as hamstrings take over the work from your tired quads. Take it slow when practicing your transition. For your first few, make sure you hydrate and fuel, especially if your workout session is over an hour. Bricks demand much effort from your body, so you need to replenish if you want to recover for your next brick session.

Tri Training

With tri training you'll also incorporate a swim, then run or swim, then a cycle brick. We suggest near the end of your swim, the last 30 seconds or so, you kick your legs a little harder to "awaken" them, get the blood flowing, and prepare yourself for the bike or run. You'll also be running into the transition after your swim, and once again after you bike as you leave the transition area to do your run. During training, Jamie enjoyed developing her brick workouts—and they became easier as her swimming skills developed. With consistent training in all areas of the tri, she began looking forward to the demands and challenges of a brick—cycling for 30 minutes, followed by a 10 to 15 minute run, gradually adding time to build endurance.

In a race, you'll transition between swimming, then cycling, and then running, so it's good to practice in that order—doing a swim-to-cycle brick, and also the cycle-to-run brick. The training program covers both types of brick workouts, as well as swim time to run to get you prepared to run into the transition.

Hope Martin, a TWT trainer and certified indoor cycling coach, learned to train her legs from transitioning from one sport to another by starting slowly, then increasing intensity and speed once her legs were stronger and she became accustomed to bricks. Hope began doing triathlons when she was 55 years old as a way to get physically fit and lose weight. Her swim coach thought triathlons would be a good fit for her because of the cross training. Now, along with competing in three to four

Hope Martin.

triathlons during the season for six years, Hope coaches 20 to 30 women a year in Sprint and Olympic distance races. She offers the following tips:

- When wearing a wetsuit, use Body Glide skin protectant around the edges of your shoes, so you can slide into shoes easily. Also apply this product to your neck, wrists, and ankles to prevent chafing from your wetsuit.
- Keep an extra water bottle on hand to clean off sand and dirt before getting onto your bike shoes or running shoes.
- Using lace locks (elastic shoestrings you don't have to tie) also saves time, since you don't need to tie your shoes.

In the training plan during the intensity phase, you'll get a taste of your first brick at Week 6. By then, you'll have a solid base of intense workouts and feel prepared to add brick workouts. Enjoy the challenge and don't forget to journal about your experiences and how your body feels.

Libby's bricks

Before my first race, I muddled through training, trying to figure out what this triathlon stuff was all about. In fact, when I did my first bike-to-run exercise, I didn't even know it was called a brick. I told my legs to run, but they didn't want to cooperate. They felt heavy and wobbly. I felt discouraged after my first brick experience and doubted my lofty goals, but to my pleasant surprise, the second bike-to-run brick was better, and by my fourth or fifth try, my legs felt much stronger. My body adjusted to my demands, and I was jumping off my bike and setting off for a run without thinking twice about it. I didn't learn the importance of fueling until much later in training, when I realized fuel is a huge part of the process. As I increased the demands on my body and learned to replenish electrolytes, I felt much better doing the demanding bricks. Now I'm not intimidated by bricks and love the feeling of being soggy on my bike. I enjoy the tingle in my legs as they figure out they aren't peddling the bike anymore, they're running.

TWT Training Week 6: Betsy's First Brick

Bricks were one of the things that intrigued me about triathlons. Cycling for miles then putting on running gear and running for more miles seemed like a true athletic endeavor. Bricks were so mysterious to me that I never considered attempting one on my own. But when I saw it on the training schedule at week six, I felt ready for it—even excited, and it was a "taste" of a brick, nothing insurmountable. I was up for the challenge—to see if I could do it and how I'd feel.

The date was Wednesday, May 21, 2008 at 6:30 p.m. as we met at Blue Star Forest Preserve bike path in Glenview for a 30-minute cycle out and back, to be followed by a 10 to 15 minute run. I had loaded all of my equipment in my car, along with plenty of water and some gels. I felt energetic and ready to go. While cycling, I kept up with the group—trying to maintain a decent speed—so by the time

I clipped out of my shoes to change into my running shoes I felt a little fatigued. How would I feel on this run? I had butterflies in my stomach, not knowing what to expect, but felt comfort from my fellow tri women, seeing them calm during our first brick. We rested our bikes on the grass, took sips of water, and ripped open our gels to gulp down. We took our time taking off our cycling shoes and putting on our running shoes, but didn't want to pause too long for fear our leg muscles would tighten and our hearts rates would slow too much.

I laced my shoes, sipped more water, and headed down the shaded path with Sue, Kim, and Stef in a slow jog. I was already warmed up from the cycle, so my heart rate was up and my lungs felt good— but my quadriceps literally felt like bricks! My muscles were wobbly until they adjusted to the run motion, but I eventually found my pace. My usual running style took over, and over the next 10 minutes I felt fine—as though I was already warmed up and on the last half of a long run. I focused on my form and talked to my fellow trainees about our legs. Yes, we all felt it. We completed the loop, then met beside our bikes to stretch.

Just put your mind and body to it, and you can do this, too!

Key Points

1. A "brick" workout consists of combining two workouts of two different sports.

2. Practice, practice, and more practice....

3. Take brick training slowly so your legs have time to adjust and your body acclimates to standing from a supine swim position.

4. Remember to refuel between sports.

5. Gradually increase speed and intensity during your brick workouts to improve endurance.

SECTION III

You Can Reach Your Peak

CHAPTER 9

Making a Smooth Transition

"The difference in the impossible and the possible lies in the person's determination."
-Tommy Lasoda

Libby's First Race Transition

EMERGING FROM THE 52-degree water of the San Francisco Bay, I glowed from my triumph over the choppy waves, completing the one and a half mile swim of my first triathlon. On this chilly spring morning I wasn't part of just any triathlon, but one of the most revered in the world: Escape from Alcatraz.

I peeled off my slippery wetsuit and jogged into the transition area, feeling my heart quicken as I approached the section where I'd racked my bike. The elite racks were bare and the ground was littered with gel and energy bar wrappers. Some athletes cycled out, while others ran in. My eyes scanned the rack for my bike, but nothing looked familiar. I couldn't wait to jump on my new Bianchi Veloche (my first bike since I was 10-years-old) and let it help me up the San Francisco hills. As I took one more panicked scan, I realized not only was I missing my bike, I didn't see the towel, running shoes, or singlet I had laid out on the ground beside my bike at 5 a.m. that morning.

Time was ticking, but fortunately I located a race official and pleaded for help. "I can't find my bike!" I panted, "Someone took my bike." The official gave me a gentle pat on the back, smirked, and asked if this was my first race. A little irked I said, "Yes, but what does that have to do with my missing bike?"

He took a quick gander at my race number on my arm and kindly walked me to my rack that matched my race number. He pointed to one of the bikes on the rack—and there it was, sparkling in the sun, my beautiful green Bianchi, my towel, shoes, water bottles, and gear bag. I turned to my new friend with a smile and said, "Thank God they returned it."

Losing your stuff in the triathlon transition area can be scary, especially early on when you're still trying to figure everything out. I took it in stride and continued the race, but learned a valuable lesson about knowing exactly where your transition "home" is located. Now this is one of the biggest tips I give our athletes: Walk the transition area. Go to the entrance of the transition as you would after your swim and trace your steps back to your home. Walk to the bike "out" and then trace your steps back to your rack and know your exit from the transition to starting your run. I do this for every single race, thanks to my mishap. I'm happy to report I've completed over 50 events without ever needing to report a missing bike in the middle of a race.

Plan and Practice Your Transition

The time it takes to transition from one sport to the next during a triathlon is known as transition time, and it's included in your total race time. In a quick snapshot, the transition area is the place you'll rack your bike (actual metal racks are set up and marked with race numbers to keep things organized) and set up your equipment to move from sport to sport. Bikes of all shapes and sizes will be racked; from thousand dollar elite tri bikes to 20-year- old mountain bikes.

In the transition area, you and all the other race participants will peel off your wetsuits (if you choose to wear a wetsuit), slip on your cycling shoes and shorts, put on your glasses and helmet, get onto your bike, exit the area to cycle, then later enter the transition area again to drop off your bike and change into running shoes. You'll exit again to begin the run segment of the race. Specific signs in the transition area are labeled "Swim In," "Bike Out," "Bike In," "Run Out," to direct you to the appropriate portion of the course. The Finish Line is in a separate area, and in a small race is typically close to the transition. The starting line, transition area, and finish line may all be far apart, depending on the race location and logistics. A map of the race course is either available on the race website and/ or in your race packet. Do check out where the Starting Line and Finish Lines are located, so you know how far you need to walk back to transition after the race to get your gear out of transition.

The key to successful transitions...

...is to think, plan, and practice moving through each transition as quickly as possible so you'll be efficient during your race, which can cut your overall time significantly. You don't need to be a gear head. Practically speaking, the less gear you have the faster you'll be. For example, in sprint distance races, you may not need socks or cycling gloves.

Practicing what works for you is the key to helping you come race day. Believe it or not, professionals typically take only 15 to 30 seconds per transition.

Newbies can make the mistake of practically eating lunch during the transition. At the end of one tri season, we recognized one TWT athlete with the "Tea Party" certificate, awarded to the one who posted the longest transition time. In this case the athlete took her time getting organized and hung out in transition for 12 minutes. She received a call from her mom while in transition in the middle of her race. Her mom wanted to know how everything was going and "Linda" gave a detailed play by play account of her experience. When it was all over and she received her tea party award, she said it was all worth it, and joked that her mom couldn't be there, but certainly was a part of her race ... and the finishing time! The following year, Linda improved her race by 14 minutes—and ten of those minutes were shaved from her previous record transition time.

One way to cut your time is to practice setting up your transition station in various ways to find what flows best for you. Organization and practice will help alleviate first race jitters.

Hope Martin, a coach and TWT trainer who races one to two times a month, says practicing transitions is an easy way to cut your over-all race times. Hope recommends that you line your gear up and practice on your own. Get in and out of your wetsuit numerous times, race without socks, and leave the biking gloves at home. If you're wearing a race belt, carry it with you and clip it on as you run to the exit, or clip it on after you get through transition. Do things as you're *moving* and don't sit down in the transition. Hope eats sports beans, GU (for quick carbs), and takes water before getting on her bike or going on the run.

Transition don'ts

Years ago, triathlon rules were more lenient. Some athletes would strip down to their birthday suit after the swim, then slip on their cycling shorts. In one of her races, Libby witnessed a man taking it all off in front of everyone without a care in the world during the swim to bike segment. Truly an unnecessary distraction! She wasn't the only athlete who added a little extra time to her race, stuck in the shock of this visual. In the end, officials penalized him and added time onto his race, for not following the rules. Just assume there is a no nudity rule in triathlons.

Don't touch or move other people's bike or gear. If someone is spread out too much and encroaching on your small space, ask them to move their things over. You wouldn't want your things moved either, so try to find the owner before adjusting someone else's gear.

Don't take up unnecessary space. Depending on the amount of people in any given race, space can be limited. Typically a small hand towel is placed on the ground under the racked wheel of your bike—this is the respectful space you should take. If you spread out your stuff, another athlete may not hesitate to rearrange your gear into a smaller area, causing confusion when you get back to your transition.

Don't forget to grab all your swim gear as you leave the transition area for the race start. This may seem obvious, but it's easy to forget something in the midst of all of the excitement. You'll pack your goggles, swim cap, (and wetsuit if you wear one) into your transition bag the night before, but you must remember to take it out before you leave transition. If transition closes and you've left your swim essentials in the area, your race may be over, because usually you can't get back in to retrieve items once the area officially closes.

Don't forget to have your fuel available and ready to eat. If you need a quick pick me up and your hands are sopping wet and cold from the swim, it's difficult to open wrappers. Have your hydration ready also. Libby once purchased a couple extra Gatorades and had them in her transition area, but forgot to take off the seal under the cap. Her options were to waste a lot of extra time removing the seals or to skip the hydration. Think through your race and come up with worst case scenarios and a rescue or action plan. If you're prepared for anything, you won't be frazzled if something comes up.

Betsy's Transition Anxiety

Since so much activity goes on in the transition area, it's no wonder athletes who've only done one-sport races experience the most anxiety over this part of the event. When I did my first race, I kept mulling over what stuff I needed, what I'd wear, what the area would look like, how I'd locate my bike, and whether I'd recognize the entrance and exits to the transition. That's why it's important to practice transitions, so you know what to expect and can become more efficient. Over time and with practice, my anxiety lessened.

I've been working on getting my wetsuit off faster—which is almost a sport in itself. Stay focused on yourself and what you need to do and your transition will go smoothly. My husband, an experienced triathlete as a young man, was confused over my fussing. "Keep it simple," he said. He never had much stuff, but just "did the race."

Libby's Rattled Bike

Almost to the highway on my way into Chicago for the Chicago Tri, I realized I'd left my bike at home. I zoomed back to my garage and quickly tossed my bike into the back of my open truck. On my way again, trying to make up for lost time, I turned a corner and heard metal on metal. I looked back in my review mirror and saw my bike had shifted from one side of the truck to the other. I hadn't taken the time to secure my bike, unfortunately, and just held my breath, not knowing what kind of shape my bike would be in when I arrived. When I finally reached the race site and took out my bike for the walk to transition, my handlebars were bent and the break wire was damaged, causing my bike to have the front wheel brakes on permanently. I frantically looked for help from friends and officials to straighten out my bike. When I finally found aide from an official who fixed my bike, I only had a couple of minutes before the transition area closed. I racked my bike, but had to leave all my gear in my bag. I completed the race but added lots of extra time, since my transition wasn't set up, and I had to get my gear out of my bag during the transitions. Race day brings a heavy dose of adrenaline, even if everything goes perfectly. Starting my race without knowing if my bike would work and knowing I hadn't adequately set up my gear at my transition home added another level of anxiety. I had to talk myself through my frustration and remind myself that some race days are better than others. I still was out there and would cross that finish line, no matter what.

COACH TIPS

Transition Set up Tips

- Start by setting up your bike in the easiest gears.
- Identify where your bike will be racked. Most transition areas have the bikes racked in numerical order. For example, athletes numbered 151 to 200 will place their bikes on a specific rack. The bikes generally don't have to be lined up numerically, just within this range and somewhere within your designated rack. If you don't see your bike right away, look down and around the rack. The posted numbers should help you find the right rack.
- Suspend your bike from the nose of the seat with the front wheel on the ground facing out.
- Place your helmet on the handle or aerobars, with your sunglasses either inside or hooked on.
- Attach your tool bag with an extra tube, CO_2 cartridge, and tire irons, underneath your bike seat.
- Make sure your water bottles are filled with water and an electrolyte drink. Some athletes freeze these the night before so they're still really cold while racing. Just be sure you have enough time for them to melt, since a frozen bottle of hydration won't do you any good.
- Place your towel (brightly colored so it's easy to see) on the ground next to your bike with your running shoes, cycling shoes, socks (optional), race belt with numbered bib, singlet (optional), and extra nutrition bars and/or gels on top. The towel is meant to help you see and locate your bike and gear. It's not typically used to dry yourself off after the swim. Plan on drip drying to save some precious transition time!
- If you decide to pre-mount your cycling shoes, this would be the time to do so.

Swim to Bike (T1) Transition

Once you've finished the swim portion of the race, you'll exit the water, jog toward the "Swim In" sign, and go straight into the transition area. During most races you'll have to do a light jog out of the swim to reach the transition area—and this is continually timed. Your final time is split to show your total time as well as your transition times.

Tips to keep you on track

- When exiting the water, pull up your goggles first.
- Use Body Glide or Suit Juice on your ankles and wrists for easier wetsuit removal.
- If you're wearing a wetsuit, as soon as you exit the water, unzip the upper half and pull it down to your waist. Once you reach the transition area you can remove the rest of your wetsuit, either while sitting down (not recommended) or standing.
- Use a little baby powder for the insides of your cycling shoes to help them slide onto your feet.
- You may want an extra water bottle to rinse off debris on your feet before you put on your cycling shoes.

You may feel some dizziness when transitioning from the swim to bike, for several reasons. For one, you're excited. Dizziness is also caused by something called orthostatic hypotension. When you immediately rise from a supine position (swimming) to an erect position (running) while demanding performance from your body, your blood pressure drops slightly, leading to dizziness. Your heart and lungs need time to catch up with the new pressure and oxygen demand. The more you practice this T1 transition, the quicker your body will accommodate this demand. As this sensation becomes familiar to you and you realize it will soon go away, you become less focused on it. If you feel extremely dizzy, SLOW your pace. Walk to transition, take relaxed deep breaths, and let your body readjust to the oxygen demand. As you take it a little easier, your pressure will adapt almost instantly and your cardiac output will start to decrease. You'll notice your heart rate slowing as your lungs decrease their workload. Your breath will become more normal and the dizziness will dissipate. Again, the more you practice swim to bike, the less you'll be affected by this natural response to the work you're asking of your body.

Transition set up on towel: helmet, sunglasses, socks, racing belt, water bottle, running shoes, visor, sports beans, cycling shoes

Bike to Run (T2) Transition

The good news is: two out of the three are done. You're off your bike and preparing for the last event. The bad news is: your legs feel like lead when you first try to run. As we discussed in the previous chapter on brick workouts, you'll experience leg weakness when moving into your run after riding the bike for several miles—and possibly several hours, depending on the length of your race. Take it slow when starting your run and give your legs time to adjust. Since you're changing sports, you might think your body would thank you with a huge burst of energy. But, once again you're asking it to perform hard work. Cycling and running use many of the same muscle groups; quadriceps, hamstrings, glutes, calves, and core. Take it slow until you get your running legs back. This is different for everyone, but in general, you'll spend the first half mile reminding your legs what running feels like. At first, assess your energy level and adjust your pace so you can make it across the finish line. Be sure you're still fueling, because you're now running on accumulated fatigue. Unless you've been diligent about meeting your fuel needs, you'll be tapping into your nutritional reserves.

COACH TIPS

Bike to Run (T2) Transition Tips

- You'll dismount your bike BEFORE entering T2, you'll cross over the timing pad and run into T2 with your bike toward your rack to get your running gear.
- Never unbuckle your helmet chinstrap before you rack your bike.
- Hang up your bike on the rack by its seat, then remove your helmet.
- Remove your cycling shoes, slide your feet into your running shoes, grab your hat (optional), race number, and belt as you're leaving, and put them on as you run out of T2.
- Using lace locks or elastic shoe laces allows you to slip your feet in easily and securely without the hassle of tying laces.
- Use a little baby powder for the inside of your running shoes to help them slide onto your feet. If you have a tendency to get blisters, slather your feet with Vaseline to prevent rubbing.
- You'll run through the transition to the "Run Out" sign to start the run portion of the race.

In one race, someone moved Libby's bike down four spots, but her towel and other gear were in their original location. Don't panic if you don't see your gear right away. Take a deep breath and look around the area, or ask for help. If you rack properly in the first place, others can help you find your gear by matching your rack to your athlete number.

Check for specific information with the volunteers or at the pre-race meetings. Well before race week, review the checklist to be sure you have all the necessary items. Of course you'll need to lay out your transition area at home, or when practicing a brick. The more familiar you are with your layout, the easier your transitions will be — and you won't be overcome with anxiety about forgetting an item.

Betsy's Tip: Flip Flops

While setting up my transition area just before my first race, I realized I had to be barefoot while I checked out the transition entrances and exits. I saw many athletes with cheap flip flops that protected their feet during the walk through and on our long walk to the swim start. This was something I should have paid attention to on the map. Racers ended up leaving the shoes at the beach and just grabbed them after the race, or left them to be donated. With each race you'll pick up what works best for you.

Don't put too much pressure on yourself in the transition during your first race. We give more tips on what to do on race morning in Chapter 12. Each practice and race is a new experience, and one in which you will learn new skills and tips.

Key Points

1. During a triathlon you transition from one sport to the next and the transition times are included in your overall race time.
2. All of your gear and equipment, extra fuel, and hydration should be racked and placed in the race transition area.
3. Plan, practice, and organize your transition area.
4. Less gear = greater efficiency
5. Swim to Bike transition is referred to as T1.
6. Bike to Run transition is referred to as T2.
7. Experiment with Suit Juice, Body Glide, baby powder, and Vaseline to help with an efficient transition from wetsuit to bike, and bike to run.
8. Focus on yourself and your space. Don't worry about the people around you.

Equipment Checklist (*denotes optional)

Swim:
Cap (the one they give you in your race packet)

Goggles (2 pair)

Swimsuit/tri suit

Wetsuit*

Cycling:
Bike

Wheels (race wheels if switching out)

Helmet

Cycling shoes

Socks*

Singlet top*

Water bottles (filled with your nutrition)

Sunglasses

Race number on bike and helmet (stickers given in your race packet at check in)

Bento box*

Seat Bag Equipment:
CO_2 inflation and cartridges*

Frame pump*

Tire irons

Multipurpose tool

Inner tube(s)

Run:
Running shoes

Socks*

Hat*

Race belt with number

Electronics:
Heart rate monitor*

Cycling computer

Transition Area:
Towel

Transition marker (i.e., balloon/flag)*

Food:

Energy bars and/or gels

Sports drink/water

Miscellaneous:

Backpack
Sunscreen
Duct tape/athletic tape
Medications
Post-race clothing
Race packet
Baby powder
Bodyglide
Bike lubricant

Tire changing equipment: tire irons, seat bag, pump, and CO_2 cartridges

Tri bike

NOTES

CHAPTER 10
Stay Motivated

"There are no shortcuts to life's greatest achievements."
-Anonymous

A NATIVE OF DURBAN, SOUTH AFRICA, Kim had lived in the United States for a year, working as a senior level manager and raising a family.

Kim Morgan

She was always athletic, ran track in grade school, played field hockey in school and as an adult, and had been a recreational runner for 26 years, but eventually grew weary of pounding out mile after mile on foot. Though she traveled for work and ran in numerous countries to experience a different cultural perspective, the loneliness of running set in and she lost the joy of hitting the trails. Longing for a new challenge, Kim began searching for ways to add variety and excitement to her exercise routine.

That's when Kim noticed Together We Tri signs at the Park Center Fitness club. The program appealed to her, because she wanted to get more involved in the community while getting fit *and* busting out of her running rut. Soon afterward, Kim met Libby at a school wellness fair. Bubbling with enthusiasm, Libby told her about TWT and inspired her to think more about doing a triathlon. Months later, Libby sent Kim an email reminding her the program would begin in a few weeks. Kim had forgotten about the program, but her curiosity was piqued again, and she decided to attend the initial meeting.

Kim says, "I didn't know what to say when we went around the room describing our goals. I didn't really understand what a Sprint or Olympic triathlon was in the United States."

Kim Begins Training

She signed up and began training in June 2008 for her first triathlon, with the late August Chicago Tri as her goal race. The first few weeks of the program she rode her "nanny bike" with the child seat on the back and a basket in the front. Other participants called her the "service provider," carrying energy bars in her basket for the crew. As Kim's training progressed, she borrowed road bikes from co-workers and friends and swam in the lake without a wetsuit. She could swim 20 lengths, but not with much confidence. Kim took swim lessons with Mary Bradbury (a TWT coach) to help fine-tune her stroke, and worked on breathing and front quadrant swimming. As she diligently practiced her swim technique, Kim increased her self-assurance in the pool. She hadn't used a wetsuit during lake swims (even cold swims), but just weeks before the Chicago triathlon she purchased a wetsuit, since she heard a cold current was coming through Lake Michigan and the waters could be choppy. Her husband Mark discouraged her from investing in too much gear, uncertain

Kim Morgan

if she'd continue with the sport. Little did he know that before long, triathlons would become a way of life for them.

Kim worked on her cycling with coach Pat Kilroy, who assisted her with shifting, pace, and cadence. Years ago as a young rider, Kim flipped over her handlebars, coming to an abrupt stop at an intersection, because her brakes weren't in good working order.[2] The accident affected her confidence on the road and in traffic. Kim was especially nervous on corners, but Pat stuck with her, riding by her side. Kim didn't have an efficient pedal stroke, either, so Pat told her about cadence—having a quick pedal stroke. With practice and putting in miles based on the training plan, Kim felt more at ease on her bike.

Having worked on her skills in her two weaker sports, Kim stayed motivated to continue training. She looked forward to applying new skills for each session and could see herself improving every day.

Race Morning Arrives

By the time race morning arrived and her alarm sounded at 4:30 a.m., Kim was ready. Her sleeveless wetsuit had arrived one week before race and she'd swam only once with it before jumping into Lake Michigan on race day. She set up her gear in transition, put on her wetsuit, and waited until 40 minutes until her swim wave was ready to walk down to the start. Music was playing and the announcer's voice boomed over the speakers. She jumped in the water with her wave, knowing she'd done everything possible to ensure a good race and a strong finish. She began swimming—finding her breath and stroke, while getting knocked around a bit by other competitors. She swam to the buoy and made the turn. As she swam back toward the city, Kim gazed into the crowd gathered on the side of the harbor and spotted her family at the water's edge. Mark had studied the course beforehand and plotted several locations to snap photos of Kim during the race and show their hand-made signs: Go Kim Go!

---

2   Always have your bike checked before riding, especially when borrowing a bike.

Kim was overwhelmingly satisfied with her race, completing the course in less than three hours. After seeing the excitement of this race, Mark jumped right into the triathlon scene and begin training for his own race.

As Kim reflects back on her first tri season, the little moments she experienced during training were most important and motivating to her: accomplishing her goal during a single workout, acquiring new skills each week, and gradually developing self-assurance and trust. Celebrating the race moments with her parents and family proved most rewarding, and that force keeps her moving forward with training. "Having discipline in all three sports helped me manage my work stress over the summer. Training helped me cope, conquer the tri, and give me strength to do everything," explains Kim.

Knowing she hasn't reached her potential, Kim is determined to improve upon her training and race times, which keeps her inspired year after year. Now, Kim and Mark enjoy training together, and triathlon has become a part of their life.

Kim's second tri season in 2009 included completing the TWT 12-week program again with a stronger base, more knowledge and motivation. After that, she decided to begin training for a Half-Ironman that November. Working with Mary—Kim and Mark put together a training schedule that would finish with the Kansas 70.3 in June.

While training, she hit a low point in March of 2010 when she fell behind during the conditioning phase of her training schedule. During this dip, the quality of her workouts dropped and she lost confidence in herself. Her rides and runs became a chore, and the joy of training fizzled out. Hitting rock bottom, Kim finally opened up to Mark and coach Mary about her difficulties. Mary reviewed Kim's travel schedule and adjusted the workouts so her long sessions were on the weekends. Discouraged from comparing herself to Mark, Kim began training separately and found other training partners who were more at her level.

Kim emerged unstoppable. With tweaks to her schedule and new training partners, her desire to keep going drastically improved. Matters brightened even more when the spring weather warmed up so she could train outside and begin working with a group.

Once Kim moved past the obstacles, she used the power of her mind to keep things in perspective. Now she encourages others to believe in themselves, make adjustments in training as needed, and find buddies to work out with.

Kim:

66 I started training for my first triathlon as a new personal challenge and to try something different. What began as a curious interest turned into a deep passion and a way of life. We all know about the physical and emotional benefits of partaking in exercise and how good it is for your body and your mind. Training for and racing in triathlons certainly ticks those boxes. An even greater benefit is the wonderful friendships and special people who've come into my life. I know they will be friends for life, and I'm so grateful to this sport for bringing us together. I'm also proud to be a role model for my two daughters, showing them how women can have a full and active life as a wife, mom, businesswoman, triathlete, and friend. 99

Mental Power

Your mental involvement in triathlons began when you decided to purchase this book and read it. You took another huge step mentally when you blocked out time in your weekly schedule to work out, then dressed and prepared for your first workout session—the 20 to 30 minute run/walk. Perhaps your decision came after weeks, months, or years of contemplation, but now you're learning AND doing, by reading this book. That's a huge step.

A specific motivation brought you to the first mental stage of training—the decision to become more fit and take on a new challenge. During this journey, remember your initial motivation and choose to think positively. As you develop mental strength for this challenge, you'll gain endurance, determination, and will power that seeps into day-to-day life, making you a leader with a positive attitude. At times, your mind may create opposition as you move through the intensity phase and reach the peak phase of training: when your workload increases and you've been training for eight to ten weeks. Be aware of this pitfall before you begin training. Our motivation always wanes at times. Just try to refocus your thoughts on the reason you committed to training and the benefits you'll reap along the way. Reaching out to others, journaling, taking time off, saying mantras, and visualization are all methods to keep you fired up with enthusiasm.

Seek Social Support

One of the best things you can do to ensure success is to enlist a buddy—a friend, acquaintance, neighbor, sibling, spouse, or significant other to train with you. Linda Burry, who has an M.Ed in Health Promotions with concentrations in Fitness/Wellness, School, and Community Health and is also a triathlete, notes that research shows people who join a team or bond with fitness friends are most likely to stay active during their entire lives. Having someone to whom you're accountable, whether it's a network, a group, or one other person, encourages you to stick with your plan.

Burry says, "Surround yourself with positive people, not basement people who make you feel horrible and load you with their problems. Choose balcony people, who see the joy in everyday life." These fitness buddies are thrilled to run in a sprinkle of rain, will notice a field of wild flowers, and will see the joy of cycling in a light snow.

As you continue building endurance with longer workouts and intensity, each day's problems will fall to the wayside as you focus on your tri sport skills and techniques. This is a compelling reason to maintain your training sessions.

Cultivate Positive Thoughts

Keeping a positive attitude and thinking upbeat thoughts during your tri journey will help you stick to your goals, bounce back from lapses, and attain results. Maintain a steady "can do" attitude toward reaching your goals, take your workouts one at a time, week by week, and you'll feel better each day.

If you encounter negative thoughts or events during the program, recording these issues in your journal will help you identify and work through them. If you start to think negatively, Burry recommends shouting "STOP!" Hearing these words will help you immediately disassociate from negative thinking. Burry also recommends keeping powerful motivational words posted around your house.

These tips will help you fight negative thinking:

- It's Monday. You work late, then ferry your children to sports events. You don't get home until 8 p.m. and there's no way you can do a 12 mile bike ride. You flop into bed at eleven and tell yourself, "I'm hopeless. This is a bad way to start the week. I'm behind already." Instead of being negative, say to yourself: "I did the weekend workouts, and last Monday I did great. I'm making progress. I'm doing this, day by day."
- It's Wednesday. You were up at 6 a.m. getting the kids getting off to school, then spent the day on work and other commitments. At 6 p.m., you think, "After this long day, I'm too exhausted for a workout." Try this instead: "I'll warm up, give myself 10 to 15 minutes to re-energize, and see what happens."
- It's Saturday morning. You're faced with a challenging hill or speed workout and think it'll be too much. Instead of worrying, tell yourself: "I'm going to enjoy this workout with my buddy, or my special time alone. I'll be doing my body good, and I'll feel stronger when I finish."

COACH TIP:

Time off matters

- The more you train, the more recovery you need.
- Take at least one day off each week to rest and get stronger.
- Do three weeks of training, then a week to recover (per the guide), otherwise you'll get burned out and discouraged.

~ Coach Hope Martin
TWT Trainer

COACH TIP:

Mantras

Reciting a mantra, a buzzword, or repeated sound can help you concentrate during a run, cycle, or swim session. Try these samples, or find another that works best for you.

- 1,2,3 (repeat).
- I am a strong/important/beautiful/Ironwoman
- Songs like "Eye of the Tiger," the theme from Rocky.
- "I will do it" "I will finish" (empowering phrases).

Libby's thoughts on motivation

I always think of my training and races as celebrations and spiritual events. I believe the time I dedicate to my health is also mental therapy—time for me to connect with nature, clear my brain of unwanted garbage, and just feel alive. When I get discouraged, I remind myself how lucky I am to have the strength, health, and desire to be a good example. If I don't want to start a workout, I look forward and remind myself how great I'll feel afterward. I can usually convince myself to take the first few steps that lead to a great workout. I find it helps to mentally break up my workout into smaller distances. "All I have to do is jog 15 minutes out, then I get to turn around and head back home," rather than thinking of a 30 minute run. During my last Ironman, I was tired after the 2.4 mile swim and the 112 mile hilly ride. I made a mental note to look at the marathon as 26 separate one-mile runs. All I had to do was reach the next water station, located at the end of every mile, then do it again and again and again. Exercise seems more doable if you mentally break it into bite-sized pieces, and soon you've gone further than you thought possible. During some races it seems nothing is coming together, but I try to concentrate on what I've done right instead of dwelling on where I missed the mark. I also think of happy times to help me through rough patches. I'll dedicate workouts to my children: a ride to Tyler, my son, or a swim to Quincy and a run to Casey, my two daughters. Just keep taking that next stroke, pedal, and step, and you'll reach your goals.

Visualization

The mind tends to wander while working out, so it's important to keep focused in a positive manner. Besides reciting a mantra that will uplift you and help your concentration, we encourage you to visualize. As endorphins release into your brain during a moderate to intense workout session, you'll experience a feel-good feeling, (another advantage to pushing yourself). This is the time to visualize yourself running tall and light on your feet. This comfortable running state is referred to as a runner's high. Exercise releases endorphins, which elevate the mood and actually have pain-relieving properties found naturally in the brain. This combination can give you a feeling of being unstoppable. But don't be discouraged if you don't feel the joy of a runner's high. Not all of us are lucky enough to have a gazelle-like run each time we go out.

Don't always run with your MP3 player, but go music-free and be alone with your thoughts. This is a great opportunity to seek a connection with a higher power and your inner self. Use this time as a meditative experience. Try to rid yourself of any negative thoughts and be grateful for what you do have. See yourself as a lean, tall, cross-country runner, flying light down the path. Imagine all the possibilities in front of you. Visualize passing milestones along the way and crossing the finish line. The accomplishments during your journey will all come together at the end. See and conceptualize the long-term rewards you'll accomplish as you experience this journey: more energy and a toned, strong, and healthy body—both physically and mentally.

COACH TIP

"Training yourself to listen to the good voices—the cheerleader within—can be difficult, but that's what you need to do. Visualization certainly helps, in any area of your life. High school was the first time I tried this. I wanted to win the 200 freestyle more than anything, so virtually every day, I closed my eyes and envisioned swimming a perfect race from start to finish: my start, turns, finish, how I felt, how I looked, my finish ... every detail. In fact, I became so good at it, my eyes opened within a second or two of my goal time, every time. Within a couple months, I KNEW I would win. This was the first and only time I've ever raced an event without ANY doubts (Yes, I did win)."

-Mary Bradbury
TWT Trainer

The Running Mind

Experiencing a *running mind* from time to time is motivating. Feeling the joy of being tall, fluid, and smooth keeps you hitting the trails for more. You might also find that running (not so much riding the bike, because you must navigate and pay attention to road traffic) opens your mind to creative thinking. Thoughts flow more freely and ideas seem to come easily. Many runners report solving problems and finding creative solutions as they run. Exercise can be therapeutic as we open our minds to thinking beyond our lives and look at the world around us. Being in our *training mind* helps us keep things in perspective.

Inside Betsy's running mind

On a cool summer morning, one day after completing the 2009 Chicago Tri, I went out for a short recovery run. My legs were sore, but a good sore from all the hard work I'd accomplished the previous day. I left my music player at home, wanting to just be in my own mind. I started from my driveway on one of my usual routes. When I began jogging slowly to warm up, I suddenly felt extremely tall. I'm only five foot four inches tall, but I felt six feet tall, and as light as a gazelle. I kept going, completely aware of my long legs I felt moving beneath me. What was happening? Was I going crazy? I thought I was nuts and all the training had unhinged my mind. But I enjoyed the feeling, kept floating, and savored my run.

Afterward, I sent Mary an email, letting her know what I'd experienced. She responded: "That was your running mind—enjoy it." I sighed with relief because I wasn't going crazy after all—at least not yet.

Libby's Ironman

Sometimes it's not all about you. Sometimes getting out of your own worries and helping someone else carries you through a race. I've had bad races that have turned out to be unforgettable. I sent this email to my friends and family after my Louisville, Kentucky Ironman race:

Hi all!!

Thank you so much for your well wishes and all the energy sent to me on race day. Lord knows I needed it.

As you know by now, my sub 14-hour race turned into a 16-hour event. It was hot and hilly and hard. Considering I was a bit under trained, I'm thrilled I made it through the course. In the end, it was phenomenal! I'm elated to have completed the race even though I was in the back of the pack.

My family was there to see me sprint across the finish line as they shouted, "Libby you are my Ironman," and "That's my sister and she's my hero." When I crossed the finish line and ran into their arms, we all shouted with excitement that I was healthy and finished.

The swim was harder than I anticipated. There was quite a current on the first mile, which made me a little more fatigued for the next 1.2, but I came out feeling ready and excited for the ride. The ride was hot and hilly—and oh how I wish I'd trained on hills. There were bodies all over the side of the course; people who hadn't hydrated well and were dehydrated and out of the race. I went through ten bottles of water and Gatorade, did 400mg of sodium per hour, and I was still behind in fluids.

My rescue bag at mile 56 containing my nutrients lacked the peanut butter sandwich (forgot to grab it out of the fridge at 4:30 in the morn), so I ate what I had in my bag—dried cherries—then got back on and started riding and drinking. At about mile 80 I started cramping a bit. I got off, asked myself if I wanted to continue, stretched, and went back to it. All along I was taking my time, knowing I just wanted to be safe and keep going.

After the 112 ride, family members were all there to encourage me on the run. Early in the run I started getting the chills, and in 97-degree weather I knew I couldn't be cold. I was either getting overheated (heat exhaustion) or a little behind on fluids. For a quick minute I considered I might not be able to catch up on fluids and continue the marathon, even at a walk. I was tired and discouraged, but then told myself: You know how to get through this. Give your body what it needs and get back out there.

So I found a walking partner and started pushing fluids, fluids, more fluids, and salt tablets until I felt better. My new walking friend was a 59-year-old man named Tim who trained for a year for the event. His entire family was there from Florida, willing him to finish. Tim needed encouragement, so we walked and talked and I helped him to mile 13 where he had to call it quits and did not finish (DNF). That was one of the hardest parts of the entire event—continuing after letting my new pal down and not being able to help him cross the finish line. But we both felt it was becoming unsafe for him and if I stayed with him much longer I wouldn't make the cut off time to finish the race.

I started running, shuffling, walking and running, shuffling, and walking the rest of the 13 miles. When I saw the lights at the end, I started sprinting—and I mean sprinting. I think I probably ran my fastest 200-yard dash ever. I felt so strong as I sprinted to the finish. As I crossed the line, I thought: Wow I feel great! I think I have more in me. That was a moment of glorious delusion. The truth is, at times that race was a huge struggle, both mentally and physically. In the end I felt strong and so grateful to cross that finish line.

I raised my arms high, yelled a big " I did it!" cried a little, and haven't stopped smiling since. Thank you all for your support. I feel certain your energy helped carry me through at times when I needed a boost. Right now I'm going to ride this high of just finishing and feeling strong and healthy.

Journaling—Tri Notes

Tracking your progress and recording how you feel so you can look back on your past workouts—the accomplishments as well as dips in motivation—will encourage you to keep training. You'll learn from your past mistakes (nutritional or otherwise), so future workout sessions will be even more efficient and positive. Log all the positive things you've experienced during your training journey, so you can look back on them to carry you through a difficult patch.

In the TRI Notes section in the back of this book, we've included inspirational quotes to keep you motivated. The more positive you feel, the more successful you will become.

Key Points

1. Think positive thoughts during your training to help you stay motivated.

2. Find a friend, co-worker, or family member to train with you. They'll help keep you accountable and successful on your journey.

3. If you have trouble getting motivated for a workout, give yourself 10 to 15 minutes to warm up and see how you feel. You'll most likely be re-energized.

4. Take time off to recover, alternating every three weeks of training with a week of recovery, as outlined in our guide.

5. Find a mantra that works for you and use it on your swim, bike, and run workouts. The mantra will keep you motivated and moving, especially during tough workouts.

6. Visualize yourself running light, crossing milestones, and achieving goals. These images will inspire you.

7. Track your progress, write in your journal, and keep notes in the back of this book. Look back at your accomplishments along your journey. You will motivate yourself.

CHAPTER 11

Feel the Tri

*"Without inspiration the best powers of the mind remain dormant.
There is a fuel in us which needs to be ignited with sparks."*
-Johann Gottfried Von Herder

ON A BONE CHILLING FEBRUARY DAY, Yvette Finegan, mom
of three, chatted in the driveway with a neighbor who was dropping
off her son from the carpool. Despite the dreary day, they hit a bright
spot in their conversation over an upcoming half marathon taking
place in the spring. Yvette's neighbor explained that she and a few
other moms were planning to run the inaugural 13.1 half marathon in
Chicago in June. She asked if Yvette wanted to join them.

Yvette Finegan

June was the month that year Yvette would turn 40, and she'd long
wanted to run a marathon around this milestone. The combination
of good company and perfect timing led Yvette to sign up and train
with a core group of four moms for the half.

Yvette began with a moderate running base. She had started
running when her youngest was a year old—just to get away and have
time for herself, with no set goal. With the support of her team, she

began a structured program, logging regular, short weekly runs with long weekend runs. Yvette successfully completed the half marathon, and with this huge accomplishment under her belt, she felt well on her way to running her first marathon. She searched online for a race that would take place in another 13 weeks—enough time for training—which happened to be the San Francisco Marathon at the end of July. Little did she know, her first marathon would fall right in the middle of her first triathlon training season.

Yvette Finegan

Yvette's group of running buddies also talked about the Glenview Sprint Triathlon, with the cycling course going right through their neighborhood. Yvette thought of actually competing in the race, but the swim portion of the triathlon was a major issue for her.

For decades the power of water had held a strong grip on Yvette's family. Two of her distant family members drowned under unfortunate circumstances, and then, terror struck deep in her parents' hearts when Yvette, only three-years old, was caught in an undercurrent while playing in a stream, causing her to nearly drown. Hoping to combat their fears, Yvette's mom enrolled her in a few swim lessons, but that wasn't enough to make her a proficient swimmer. As she grew up, her parents didn't allow her to play in the pool with other children, feeling it was too dangerous.

Thirty-five years after her first swim lesson, Yvette dipped her feet in the water to swim, because she wanted to compete in the Glenview Tri later in the summer of 2008. Thinking she'd swim a few laps to practice for the tri, she got in the pool and pushed herself off to swim freestyle. To her surprise, her feet kept sinking. Unsure of how to become more buoyant, she struggled to swim across the pool, realizing she wouldn't have the confidence or ability to do the triathlon that year.

Yvette's Determination Prevails

She didn't abandon swimming, but enlisted a friend to come with her once a week for support. To her dismay, her feet still kept sinking and her breathing remained uneven and labored. After struggling for six months, she saw fliers about the TWT program and decided to sign up for the TWT 12-week program. Yvette's initial goal was to train for the Glenview Sprint Triathlon, which had a pool swim, with no swimming in the lake. However, it would take place on the same weekend as the San Francisco Marathon she'd committed to running. She had to shift her thoughts around and re-set her goal to do the Chicago Triathlon at the end of the summer—which *did* include a lake swim.

With instruction from Mary Bradbury (head coach for TWT), she worked on body positioning and kicking drills with and without a kick board. She kept up her regular runs and cycling sessions, following the 12-week plan, while continuing to develop her swim stroke and comfort level in the water.

Yvette brought all of her gear—wetsuit, goggles, swim cap, bike, helmet, cycling shoes, sunglasses, towel, running shoes, and water—down to Chicago's lake front to practice doing all three sports together. The group met before the Chicago Triathlon for a "mini-tri" Chalk Talk (review of the race) at a grassy area near the race start. This included a low intensity half-mile swim, a 12-mile bike (six miles for sprint distance racers), and a two-mile run (one mile for sprinters). Yvette hadn't set up a transition before and had no clear idea what to do.

In transition, she watched others and listened to the coaches describe how to set up her area: placing her helmet on her bike handlebars, her sunglasses on the ground near her bike shoes. She finished the mini-tri learning more about transitions: heightening her awareness of the sequence during transition, learning the importance of practice, laying out her gear, and trying not to forget her sunglasses in T1.

Yvette says, "Everything is so short when doing the mini-tri, so it emphasizes your weaknesses. You shouldn't go into the triathlon without doing this first. It's essential. It gave me an idea of what the experience was going to feel like." She went on to complete the Chicago Olympic Triathlon, feeling well prepared for both transitions. She still struggled with the open water swim; even the slightest things sent her into a panic or bothered her, like water going up her nose, somebody bumping up against her while swimming, the waves created by a mass swim, and not being able to see the bottom. The sensation of having her face in the water seemed overwhelming at times. But Yvette didn't give up. She kept working on her swim stroke, slowly gaining confidence in the water.

She was proud of her athletic accomplishments the year she turned 40. When the season ended, she'd completed a Sprint and Olympic triathlon, a half marathon, two marathons, as well as two 5K races.

Yvette started the following year looking forward to lake swims, finding them relaxing and not thinking twice about the murky water. She learned how to swim and overcome her fears. She was beyond satisfied. She continued improving with each session, and by each race day was ready for the water, no matter what conditions the day brought. When she completed her race in Chicago, she was so excited about the accomplishment that she felt compelled to go back and help a few of her fellow TWT athletes complete their run. It was a 90-degree day and she knew the support would be appreciated. Helping others during their race lifted her spirits and became one of her favorite moments. She'll be back for more.

Yvette:

❝ I'm a big believer in life lessons being learned through sports. That being said, attempting to do a triathlon was more than this middle-aged mom just trying to find her inner athlete. If that was the case, I'd have stayed in the comfort of my newly found world of running and stretched my athletic prowess by running marathons. Attempting a triathlon was about conquering my fears in a swarm of swimmers in a lake, battling the lost identity of being a stay at home mom, and finding the courage to get out of my comfort zone and to try something I might fail at (I couldn't swim). The confidence I gained after completing my first triathlon was overwhelming. I achieved what seemed to be impossible. However, the most unexpected and rewarding life lesson came from the wonderful people I met along the way. While triathlon is not a team sport, I formed unique bonds with fellow training colleagues. These bonds are different from my other friendships in life and go beyond the shared sweat, sacrifice, and joy that go into the daily grind of training for the big day.

Since I tend to sometimes enjoy training more than the actual race day, these relationships mean more to me than the accomplishment of completing a race or setting a personal record. These sometimes brief, but strong, shared connections with people are what keep me doing more triathlons and marathons. That and the fact that I continue to work out my inner battles with life through swimming, biking, and running. ❞

Putting it All Together

In the final few weeks of the training schedule, two Saturdays are set aside for a mini-triathlon. These are designed for you to practice all three sports in sequence and go through T1 and T2. Essentially, you get to apply everything you've been training for over the past ten weeks. The idea is to use this time to focus on your transitions, rehearse your hydration and fuel methods, wear your racing gear to be sure it fits and feels right before you actually race, and work on any weaknesses or glitches prior to race day.

If you're doing this on your own, two weeks before your race try to go to the race site and walk or run the run course, then cycle the bike course. Print out the map of the course, which is usually available on the race web site. Sometimes the cycling turns in the road can be difficult to find. Even if you don't get them all correct, you'll have a general idea of the course. If you can't run or cycle the course, driving it is also beneficial. At least you'll know if the course is hilly or flat and where sharp turns occur.

Find the transition area so you'll know exactly where it's located. Enlist a friend or two to go with you on a weekend morning or early evening when the streets aren't busy. It's also a good idea to check out the parking area—whether it's an open lot or you'll need to use nearby parking garages. Gauge the time you'll need to park and walk to the transition.

If you can't do a mini-tri at the race site, at least try to do a swim-bike-run transition dress rehearsal near a local pool. You can set up your transition outside the pool area or near your car, so you can lock your bike or put it in your car. This will take extra time, but you'll still be able to practice moving from the swim, bike, and run in sequence. This practice session is one of the most important steps to make sure you're race ready. We've seen far too many athletes arrive on race day without ever putting all three sports together. They experience far more problems than the people who've done a dress rehearsal.

Sample Mini-Tris for TWO weeks before the race:

- *Sprint distance mini-tri:* 10-15 minute warm-up swim in the lake if possible, followed by an easy 1/3- to ½-mile swim, then a 10-12 mile moderate difficulty bike ride, then a 1-mile sprint run followed by a 1-mile easy run. Practice your transitions and build on your intensity in each segment of the tri.

- *Sprint distance mini-tri:* warm-up, then swim 20 minutes, bike 35 minutes, and run for 10 minutes.
- *Olympic distance mini-tri:* warm-up, then do a 40 minute swim, bike 50 minutes, and run 20 minutes.

Libby's Mini-Tri Chalk Talk

During our last training session a few days before race day, we always meet for a question and answer session. Most of the questions involve things we've already covered, such as how many folks are in each wave (varies depending on the race—may be 20 or 100) and how often each wave goes off (typically every 3 minutes). These are things worth knowing before your race. You can find this information on the race website or by going to your specific race Q and A session held at packet pick up. We make sure everyone has their race swim cap and knows what wave they're in and what time their race starts. We print off the maps and do a visual walk through. Do a mental, or in person walk through of the race course and start physically prepping for your race.

Be reassured it's good form to taper your training the week before the race, even though you may feel guilty about taking it easy. You've already done all the work, including dress rehearsals. You're ready. There's nothing more you can do, so sit back, relax, and start thinking positively about your race. Begin hydrating and make sure you eat well. Also remember to sort out your gear and nutrition, refer to your gear list, and review it twice. Our groups always meet for a morning picture and to discuss logistics regarding where we want to meet after the race. This would be good for you to plan as well. You've worked hard for this day, so make sure you have someone to document your amazing accomplishment and you've given your family and friends guidelines to spot you. Write out your timeline like this:

My race starts at 7:20 a.m., swim exit 7:40, five minute T1, bike out at 7:45, bike back in at 8:35, T2 three minutes, run out 8:38, cross the finish line 9:15 a.m.

With these guidelines, family and friends can look for you, keeping in mind the times are approximate. Since you've been training, you should have a handle on how long each segment will take on race day. If you're realistic with your times, people will probably be able to spot you several times throughout the race. You've done the work, now get ready to enjoy your moment!

Key Points

1. Visit the race website to download the course map. If possible, visit the race site to either drive the bike course or ride and run the bike and run courses.

2. Put the skills you've developed all together by doing a mini-tri at two weeks before your race. You'll practice transitions and get the feel of what it will be like to do a triathlon. Remember all your gear!

3. When you do your mini-tri, be sure to practice hydration— keeping in mind your race will be longer.

4. Wear your gear during the mini-tri practice sessions to be sure it fits and feels right.

5. Take notes on what you learned during your mini-tri session, including what you ate before and how you felt.

SECTION IV

Time to Taper

CHAPTER 12

Get Race Ready

*"Focus on the journey, not the destination.
Joy is found not in finishing an activity but in doing it."*
-Greg Anderson

ON A TUESDAY EVENING in April, Eileen Neville arrived for her first tri training session at the Chicago Park District's quarter mile loop track near her home. Wearing a pair of new running shoes, Eileen shuffled around the track, stopping to catch her breath before she did a full lap. Also at the track were Carrie and "Susan" (not her real name). Carrie, a thin, fit runner, cruised around the track effortlessly, while Eileen and Susan chatted as they alternated between a run and a walk.

Eileen Neville

Six months earlier, with an extra 50 pounds on her five foot six inch body frame, Eileen investigated triathlon training in an effort to lose the weight she gained while on bed rest during her second pregnancy. Eileen had been an avid downhill skier (skiing 50 to 60 days a year), played ultimate Frisbee for two years, and player soccer in high school. Despite starting her tri journey without being able to swim a single lap or run, she set a goal of finishing a triathlon.

Her husband agreed to come home from work early on Tuesday evenings so Eileen could train. As soon as she could leave the house, Eileen would jump on her bike and sprint to the gym to train.

She reports, "I was so happy to be training and making new friends. Getting out of the house to exercise was an accomplishment in itself." She kept up her run/walk routine, gradually building a base and decreasing her walk time with rests in between. During week two of training, she was able to complete over two miles in a walk/

Eileen Neville

jog, with a short rest in between. Each week Eileen added miles, still keeping a slow pace. By the fourth week she was able to run three miles continuously at a slow, steady pace.

As Eileen followed the training schedule she began losing weight and feeling better about herself. Working toward a triathlon and doing something for herself brought self-esteem. She enjoyed time with her family and developed more patience with her kids, knowing she'd have a break at the end of the day from preparing meals, cleaning up messes, and interacting with her children. At the end of the day, Eileen would get to swim in the lake, do her favorite run, or ride her bike.

With 12 weeks of diligent training behind her, race day morning arrived—her first Chicago Triathlon. With her stomach twisted into a ball full of nerves, Eileen bundled up her long hair, slipped on her skintight swim cap, and huddled with her start wave of racers. Susan, her new training friend, was one of them. When the announcer said it was time for their wave to jump in Lake Michigan with 50 or so other women to tread water before the start, she and Susan jumped in. They hugged tight, gave each other high five's, and before they knew it, the horn sounded. Off they swam, bumping into other swimmers, finding their freestyle pace for 1.5 kilometers to start off their first Olympic distance race. Susan finished the swim ahead of Eileen and decided to wait at the swim exit, watching for her to come in. When Eileen came to the exit, Susan pulled her out of the water saying, "Come on girl, let's go!" They ran together to the transition. Eileen was thrilled Susan waited for her. On her bike she pumped her legs hard on Lake Shore Drive, doing the designated two laps. During the run she saw Libby racing, and they cheered each other on. She was elated as she crossed the finish line and met her husband Andy and the kids. The children wore white t-shirts with the logo: Go Mommy Go! on the front. On the back were drawings of a person swimming, biking, and running. One shirt on the back said, "No drafting."

After the Race

Eileen grabbed some water, proudly accepted her finisher's medal, and found the TWT tent. Susan came to find Eileen to tell her she heard she'd won something—she finished third place overall in the mountain bike division! Eileen won a huge packet of stuff and was on a high forever. To top it off, race day was her wedding anniversary, so she and Andy celebrated the day with a special dinner in the city.

Eileen recalls having a "wow" conversation in her head and with her husband. She realized she could hold onto this third place finish and be proud, or she could take it to the next step and consider buying a road or triathlon bike. She decided to keep on going. She shopped forever for a road bike, unsure whether to get a tri or a road bike. She finally found a great deal on a tri bike and went for it.

Eileen, now an experienced racer, advises, "On race day, keep things simple. Your gear doesn't need to be fancy, but you need to know how to use it. I also recommend you don't get caught up in other people's game. Try NOT to stress out!"

She learned from mistakes while racing. She once stopped on the racecourse, wondering where the other athletes were. Conversing with the volunteers at a water station, and drinking water she asked them if she was in the right spot. As she chatted she lost valuable time. (She says her mind was elsewhere. She wanted to be with her brother in New Jersey, at his police academy graduation that day. She found out later she missed placing third by just 20 seconds).

Eileen has enjoyed sharing her lifelong achievements by transforming from meager beginnings to developing into a stellar athlete. Her rise to success made her tri training an extremely positive experience. After her first year of tri training, Eileen coached the women's TWT group to inspire others and pass on her knowledge. She continued as a trainer for three more years. She also watched what she ate, lost a few more pounds, gained strength, and competed in several sprint triathlons. That year she learned about completing the work (got her kids organized so she could get out of the house to practice as laid out in the 12-week program) to get to the finish line. She also learned doing the program and racing isn't scary. You're actually racing yourself, with other people around you in stages of their own personal races. The people she trained with were truly her companions rather than competitors. She also discovered the transition wasn't free time and needed to be as simple and fast as possible. Eileen's run was always her shortcoming, but she learned to make up for it in her transition times by being smart and practicing.

Eileen kept up her training even in the off-season (more on off-season training in the appendix), which helped her improve from year to year. During the off-season, she likes to focus on Pilates and yoga, along with conditioning her body to keep up with the swim, bike, and run events.

With perseverance, practice and repetition, Eileen propelled herself to doing Half Ironmans and even placed on the elite team.

She began doing cyclocross (cross-country bike racing on a course), training consistently, and competed in ten races during her first season. She went on to win the state championship race and became a small group cycling coach, sharing her expertise, and cheering others on to accomplish their athletic goals.

Eileen:

66When you do something for yourself, the rewards are ten-fold. You start to feel better about yourself, you're more patient, and it makes you a stronger person. Over the years, the consistency, repetition, and practice are beneficial. Even better, you can show your children that with repetition and practice they can reach their goals and do almost anything. 99

The Week of the Race: Taper Week

Race week is here at last, and you've prepared your body for the big day. Like Eileen, you followed the training plan, practiced with your gear, and learned tips and trade secrets on your journey so you're well prepared.

The taper is typically done once per season, and with the 12-week program your main race comes at the end of that time period. This final week is when you take time to let your body rest and refuel itself. Workouts for the week are short and moderate to conserve energy. Especially for first timers, we want less than race pace, with low intensity. The last thing you want to do is pull a hamstring on a short intense run just before race day. For more seasoned athletes we recommend more intensity, but a moderate pace and passive taper is best for first timers.

Be sure you try to get sufficient rest during the week, day and night. Aim for quality sleep each night of the week to help restore and repair your body. Try to sit, and stay off your feet as much as possible, cut back a bit on eating, since you'll be burning fewer calories with shorter workouts, seek the shade, and drink plenty of water (especially when it's humid). Be sure to stretch after your workouts to help prevent injuries and keep you limber. Find time to do some things you enjoy—read a book, watch a movie, visit with family or friends. You've worked hard so enjoy some relaxation.

Race Weekend: 48 Hours Before Race Day

With just 48 hours to go before your race morning, you'll have some last minute things to do. No workouts are planned in the schedule, so it's time to pack your race bag and lay out your gear and check everything at least twice. Try to get a good night's sleep, if possible.

On Friday or Saturday you'll pick up your race packet and instructions with race numbers for your bike, helmet, and run. You'll also get a swim cap—usually a certain color designated for your specific wave. Tri races are organized in WAVES: groups that go off at different times. These are typically structured in age groups and sometimes gender. For instance, Wave 1: female 25-29 age group, Wave 2: male 25-29, Wave 3: female 30-34, and so on. Wave starts can vary, with some races having you jump in and tread water before the start alarm sounds, while others let you wait on the shore or stand in shallow water before starting the race. Some races have multiple waves with the same color swim cap, so it's important to pay attention to your wave start time, rather than only relying only on your swim cap color.

Don't spend too much time on your feet at the race expos, as you'll want to conserve energy whenever possible. You can also get body marked at the Expo. Volunteers are available to write your race number on your arms and legs in black permanent marker. Body marking can also be done race morning, but allow a few extra minutes to wait in line. In order to race, you must have your race numbers visibly written on your arms and legs.

Once you've gone through your race bag, put your number on your helmet and bike. You can pin your bib number to a singlet (a light, sleeveless run shirt) for your run or put it on a race belt that you clip on in T2. Pack these in your bag along with your cycling and running shoes, socks (optional), a towel, goggles and nutrition, such as high carb gels, gu's, and of course, water and/or an electrolyte drink. Fill your water bottles the day before and put them in your fridge, or even the freezer.

During the days leading up to your race, eat plain, easily digestible food such as whole grains, peanut butter, oatmeal, and bananas. Don't focus much on wheat and vegetables, which can cause gas and an upset stomach (remember our tips in Chapter 5). *Don't try any new or spicy foods the night before or the day of the race.* Drink plenty of water a couple of days before the race to pre-hydrate your body to prepare for long, demanding exercise. Don't let yourself get thirsty during the few hours before the race—that's imperative!

As you get ready for bed, think about all of your accomplishments on this journey and how far you've come. Be confident you will complete the race feeling great! You have your race and nutrition plan, and now it's time to rest. Lastly, be sure to set your alarm to awaken you early enough to eat, drive, park, and set up your things in transition 30 to 40 minutes before it closes. With your plan in place, you're ready to race!

....

Betsy's TRI with ME Blog post August 29, 2009
EXPO Buzz, packet pick-up and final touches

Now we're only hours away from the fun! Yvette, Pam, and I headed into Chicago for an early packet pick up. We arrived by 9 a.m. with no lines yet at the Expo. We heard yesterday when it opened at 3 p.m. the lines were outrageous. By going early and staying about an hour, we took care of what we needed (packet pick up and getting our wave times), saw a few TWT friends, shopped, and visited a few booths. We didn't want to tire ourselves walking around for too long.

My race time tomorrow was 6:54 a.m.—sprinters go first. I decided to do the Sprint distance to get an earlier start time, because I didn't feel I had time to train for the Olympic distance.

Anyway, we were able to get in a bit of shopping—great deals on any kind of sportswear you can imagine. Sun glasses, tri shorts, goggles, you name it. We were considering swim skull caps made of wetsuit material to keep our heads warm in the water, but the chin straps seemed too tight. Instead, we decided to bring an extra swim cap and layer up if it's cold in the morning. One of our friends did end up buying a skullcap, so we'll see how she likes it if she uses it.

Now at home, I've worked down my checklist and assembled my gear. Yvette and I are driving down tomorrow way before sunrise. At this point, I felt prepared and plan to enjoy the race—race hard, of course, but enjoy it.

I found photos from last year's event and saw my HUGE smile at the end. I recall being nervous and scared the day before, one year ago, and then at the wave line-up I felt relaxed and ready to get started. In the end, I remember the feeling of accomplishment and the fun I had … bringing me back again this year.

Race Morning

Race morning will bring excitement, anticipation, and some nervousness—all natural feelings. Remember to go with the flow of the race and focus on each segment with strength and determination, plus a smile, and you'll have a rewarding experience.

Once you reach the transition area, find your space on the rack, hang your bike by the seat, and lay out your gear. You MUST HAVE YOUR BIKE HELMET in order to race. If you forget it, you won't be allowed to start the race. Become familiar with your surroundings. Look around and count how many racks you are from the swim exit and then from the bike in. You should walk through the transition, from the swim exit to your gear, from the bike entrance to your rack, and to the run exit. In a large triathlon the transitions can be stressful, so walking through before the race helps your prepare and stay calm when you enter T1 and T2 during the race. Try not to get caught up in everyone else's hype and nervousness. Don't worry about what's in their gear bag or let their chatter throw you off and make you nervous. Everyone comes from a different background and has a unique perspective.

Once you've set up your transition area, you can either put on your wetsuit there, or exit with your swim essentials: swim cap, goggles, and wetsuit. This decision depends on your wave time and how far you need to walk to the starting line. If you have an hour or more before your start time, you might consider waiting to put on the wetsuit. Waiting in a wetsuit can get hot, so plan accordingly.

Once you're out of transition and waiting for your wave start time, you can eat a high carb snack and relax, and take any items to gear check. Most races have a supervised gear check area for a small bag that may contain your car keys, phone, money, a few snacks, extra water—any items you might need right after your race and before you can get back into transition. After your gear is all checked and you're start time approaches, we recommend you warm up in the water.

Your pre-race packet information will list when the water will be open for warm ups, so be sure to reach the water in time to get your face wet, loosen up, and swim a few strokes and drills. This will help calm your nerves and allow you to focus on your race. If the water is cold, you'll be able to acclimate to the temperature so it won't be such a shock to your system when you start racing. Ideally, warm up for 15 minutes. You can also jog to the swim start for 10 minutes, if possible, adding in a few accelerations to help your body kick into racing mode.

You're Out There Racing: On the Course Tips

While you're racing, keep a few tips in mind to help your race go smoothly. These rules of thumb will help you feel confident and prepared. You've already practiced these tips during your training and with the mini-tri run through, so your body is familiar with race pace.

- Start slow on the swim and focus on long strokes and finding your breathing pattern and pace. Remember to sight about every ten strokes.
- When you begin biking, start pedaling at a high cadence or easy gear/tension, with a quick leg turnover to find your cycling legs and prepare them for a long ride.
- On the run, you already know your legs will feel like bricks, so start slow and gradually build to a comfortable race pace.
- Don't forget water! Remember you'll be sweating. Check in with your nutrition plan every 15 minutes or so to hydrate and refuel.

Cross the *Finish Line* with a smile and the powerful feeling of accomplishment! You completed your journey—you're now a TRIATHLETE!

CONGRATULATIONS!

After the Finish Line: Take Care of Yourself, You Deserve It!

While you munch on carbs after your race (remember to eat something within 30 minutes of crossing the finish line), be sure to stretch your lower and upper body. You've demanded a lot from your whole body for the past few hours, and stretching your hamstrings, quadriceps, calves, and arms will help prevent tightness and heavy lactic acid build up. If there's an option to get a massage after the race in a post-race tent, do it! Massage therapists are often onsite to do massages, which helps decrease lactic acid build up and prevent soreness. Compression sleeves worn on your calves also aid in recovery. You can find these online or at a running store. They reduce muscle fatigue, damage, and increase circulation. Continue hydrating throughout the rest of the day.

When you get home, take an ice bath to help prevent soreness. It's not comfortable, but this is one of the best ways to decrease muscle swelling. After a good night's rest, take an easy day with passive activity and possibly a massage. Focus on drinking water throughout the day to help restore and recover your fatigued muscles. An Epsom salt (magnesium) bath can also relieve sore and tired muscles. You deserve pampering!

Tri Notes

Remember to document your moments: take pictures and journal about your first triathlon experience, writing about the details of the day so you can relive your special moment any time. You'll soon realize how this journey enhances other areas of your life.

....

Betsy's TRI with ME *blog post, September 28, 2009*
Ending the tri season on a high note with the Danskin Tri at Pleasant Prairie, WI

The fog lifted and the sun peeked out for a few minutes at 7 a.m. yesterday, Sunday, just in time for the Pro and Elite groups to make their splash into Lake Andrea in Pleasant Prairie, WI, kicking off the Danskin Tri—the last of the series this year.

Nervous and excited women gathered for the last triathlon of the season. The crowd of about 1,100 women was half the 3,000 who raced last year when the event was held in June. Nonetheless, our bikes were crammed on the racks with little room to spare. This was my fifth triathlon, so I felt confident, prepared and relaxed. I checked in with other TWT racers, enjoying the camaraderie and high energy level of the transition area.

Since we had a long walk down to the beachfront start, I jogged it. I stayed mostly on the grass next to the paved path, but still felt small stones jabbing my feet. At the beachfront, the water was open for a swim warm up. I put my feet into the warm water (70 degrees or so) and splashed a little. With music rockin' to get us revved up,

I lined up for Wave 9 around 7:22 a.m. A TWT friend approached with a nervous look in her eyes, saying she hadn't swum much in the past three weeks. I said, "You'll do fine. Just pretend you're at Valley Lo with the group on a Tuesday night." She smiled, but still looked uneasy. We started the swim next to each other and I told her, "Good luck and have fun!"

With the swim, I tried to stay on the right edge, but found myself drifting toward the middle of the pack. I didn't want to be there. I tried to steer back to the edge and almost ran into a large orange inflatable buoy. Oops! I felt good in the water, not sighting much, but focusing on my form, breathing on both sides to keep my rhythm.

Out of the water, I ran. I had a little trouble pulling off the arms of my wetsuit, but kept jogging as I fought it off. Areas of the bike route were beautiful, but we had several turns followed by uphill climbs that slowed us all down. I passed two women chatting on their ride and another who said, "Whoa, I'd better get out of your way!" Hey, wasn't this a race?

I was into T2 and feeling good, my legs a little numb from pushing them, plus the cold. I put on my running shoes, cut across the grassy median, and headed out for the run—a flat course. A few guys on the sidelines saw my number 800 and shouted "Go 800!" and gave me a high five. Another shouted, "Go Together We Tri!" since I had on my TWT tri suit. These words of encouragement helped me run faster. I kept telling myself: "Relax, run tall, relax your shoulders and arms, this is a nice Sunday run." Another runner came up to pass me and said quietly and personally, "Good job, way to go, keep it up!"

I said back, "Good job!" I recognized her from my start wave. As I ran toward the finish line, a few TWT members spotted me and shouted encouragement. I yelled back at them, breaking the silence in the air. All the runners were working hard toward the finish. Running down the final stretch I saw the racer who whizzed by me on her bike. She was done and gave me an encouraging thumbs up as I passed.

At the finish gate, Sheila, the pro swimmer who kicked off the race, stood in front off me with her hand out to high five, and said with a big smile, "Way to Go!" Her encouragement and excitement for every racer is what makes Danskin unique. You never feel you're alone in your quest to finish the race.

Soon after I finished, I heard two more names of TWT friends finishing. YES! What a great feeling to hear familiar names in such a big race. I was thankful for the day, the event and great people. Everyone who finished was a winner!

Libby's Third Ironman, September 12, 2010

My inner athlete was still alive and thriving—ready to take on another Ironman distance. Over the years, starting with my first dream of becoming a triathlete back in San Francisco, my passion has continued to burn. Training remains an adventure I love and enjoy each day.

With my third Ironman, I knew what I was getting into. I've never been a super-fast athlete, nor do I aspire to be in the top of any category. I don't want to risk a mishap that causes me to DNF, and I do want to enjoy my moments. That's my basic agenda for each race.

Each course has different challenges, plus the weather is never entirely predictable and each of us has days where we feel strong and days when we don't. My confidence and training level going into this race were subpar. Despite that fact, I still believed I had the strength to get started and keep going—if I made it to race day.

A recent medical issue took me to the emergency room six days before the race. After a CT scan, a new diagnosis of trigeminal neuralgia, and a new medication, I went on my way, unsure of what the coming days would bring.

As with any Ironman, athletes must check in on the Friday before the race, check their bikes by midday Saturday, and attend a mandatory prerace meeting on Saturday night. Without those steps, you are out before the race even starts. After much debate, Craig and I decided I should at least go through the motions. So, I drove up Friday with my friend Nancy and went through check in.

The excitement and expectations at these events are palpable. You hear folks bragging about PR's and how many Irons they have under their belt, while others are happy to just survive the race. Looking around, you realize everyone has put major effort into this day—hours of training, guilty runs while feeling the imposition on family, blisters and saddle soreness, sweat and tears. You meet people with incredible stories and high hopes. The excitement and expectations at one of these events is palpable. It's an awesome and very alive environment. You begin to feel as if everyone is in this thing together. You meet people with incredible stories, journey's and hopes surrounding the big day. It becomes an "Iron Family", who all wish each other well and can't imagine the disappointment should any one of these fellow athletes not be able to reach the end and cross the finish line.

As race day approached, I still wasn't sure I could participate. Before going to bed on Saturday night, I called Craig and we talked about this race being a celebration. We decided, why not give it a try? I learned a long time ago that my value is not determined by my performance, appearance, or position in this world. I'm still Libby whether I start this race and don't finish or whether I decide not to do the race at all. It doesn't change my value in this world one bit. I would take the course hour by hour and just enjoy the day.

The race turned out to be a wonderful experience. The swim was crowded but refreshing, and the ride ridiculously hilly. During the first round of major hills around Mile 40, about halfway to the top, the crowd started cheering. The applause grew louder and the excitement built as I ascended. Moments later, the motorcycle and lead pro racer passed me, then the next pro, then the next. Someone pointed to me and announced "There's the first female, leading the pack." And then quickly, "Oh, no—maybe not!" I had to laugh as the professionals zipped past me to finish their second loop of the race. I had a few moments of glory, being mistaken as one of the pros.

The best part of my race and my most special memory occurred at mile twelve of the run, when a man jumped onto the course ahead of me, waving his arms above his head and shouting, "Go, Libster, go!" With a huge smile and tears I said to myself "That's my Craig, that's my Craig! I can't believe he made it." I ran to him gave him a double high five and a kiss. He said, "No time for PDA... You are rockin this...Get goin' Hon."

I was on some euphoric cloud after seeing him and felt no pain for the next ten miles. He tracked me down at miles 14, 16, 18 and 20 to tell me how strong and amazing I was. He became my personal cheerleader, the person I wanted there for me more than anyone. At mile 18 I told him how difficult it was getting to convince myself to keep running, but he said, "I know, but that's never stopped you before. I'll see you at the finish." And he was right. Hard has never stopped me. So I just kept going: hard is only a frame of mind! I ran my fastest marathon time. Thanks to my biggest fan—I wouldn't have traded that surprise for the world.

When I finished, I celebrated! I had the health, the strength, the will, and Craig, to carry me through. And on top of it all, I had the love, cheers, and well wishes from all my friends and family who were with me in spirit.

When I got home, my children Tyler, Quincy, and Casey waited for me with posters saying "Iron Mom!" and "Go, Mom, Go!" When they kissed me and asked if I won, I showed them my medal and said "Almost sweethearts, almost!"

I thought to myself: I did win, in every way that counts.

Key Points

1. Taper Week is the week before a race when planned workouts are short and moderate, but with intensity.

2. During this week, stay off your feet as much as possible and go through your equipment check list to be sure you have everything and it's all in working order.

3. Go online to read through the course rules and review the course details.

4. The weekend before the race, try to get a good night's sleep on Friday, pick up your race packet on Saturday, and review the contents to be sure you have everything you need—including your race numbers, timing chip (if they give you one), and your official swim cap.

5. RACE MORNING: Leave plenty of time to eat, travel, and set up your transition at the race site. Stay calm and don't get caught up in the hype. Warm-up and HAVE FUN RACING!

CHAPTER 13

Enjoy Your Success!

"Go confidently in the direction of your dreams,
live the life you've imagined."
-Henry David Thoreau

YOU ARE NOW A TRIATHLETE! You've taken the TRI journey and accomplished the unthinkable: set a goal, trained, and completed a triathlon. Congratulations! Now, give yourself time to relish your accomplishment and celebrate your journey with your triathlon or workout buddy, friends, and family. This is the time to share race stories with others, either face to face or online at www.trithejourney.com.

Take a look back in your TRI Notes and read your journal entries. Reflect on what this journey has meant to you, how you've transformed, and how this accomplishment touched other people in your life. Then write in your journal about how you gained confidence in yourself; you're ready to soar to new heights. Crossing that finish line was only the first step in discovering your full potential.

With the race no longer a focal point in your life, as it was for three months, you may wonder what to do next. Expect to feel out of sorts for a few days after your triathlon, because you'll miss the structured workouts and training. You've been on this track for a full season, and now it's time to let go. Plan a recovery week with an easy run, bike, or swim with a friend or family member. Enjoy the freedom of spending the day without a specific plan. After a passive week or two, jump right back into working out for your next goal.

With the end of your program, consider your next step. Running races are still on the agenda for many triathletes who find themselves in great shape to complete a 5k or 10k run. Or sign up for a fun run with your friends and family. That's always a great way to wind down your season. Don't allow yourself to go back to your old way of life. We've seen athletes who had to start all over again the following season because they regressed to unhealthy habits and didn't exercise. We've also provided Off-Season training suggestions to guide you through the fall and winter months. The main goal is to keep motivated and moving. No matter if you choose Pilates, yoga, or boot camp—although we'd love for you to keep a few tri-focused workouts in your regimen. Off-Season is about working on your weaknesses and gaining strength. How you decide to do that is less important than the fact that you're still moving and building a stronger base. Near the end of your Off-Season training and the beginning of the next Tri season, be sure to open up this book again and use it as a guidebook for your next tri training experience. Plan for upcoming races and build on your strong base, knowledge, and experiences from last season. Review your previous year's journal notes and take them into account for your upcoming year.

Things you gained during your tri journey experience, including self-confidence and inner strength, as well as physical strength, will spill over into your daily life. This happened for each of the women featured in this book. Be sure you share your story with others, so you can inspire women who are starting the journey.

More Success Stories - Maura Kennedy: The Courage to Move Forward

During an unusually warm week of 80-degree temperatures in April of 2002, Maura Kennedy, a 35 year-old mom of three from Glenview, Illinois, noticed a red rash on her skin after being in the sun. For the next few weeks she felt exhausted all the time and remained in a fog throughout the day. Along with the utter exhaustion, Maura noticed pain in her hands and joints. Cracking an egg to scramble for breakfast was painful. Pouring her morning cup of coffee and lifting her warm mug to her lips seemed to take minutes rather than a thoughtless few seconds. During the day when she took the kids to swim in the pool, she pulled them out early because she was so tired. She sat in her car, kids in the back, and prayed to God she could safely drive her family home.

Maura believed the fatigue and pain would all go away, but things got worse. Her appetite waned as she craved sleep more than food, losing 10 to 15 pounds without even trying. Workouts on the elliptical machine lasted only a few minutes. Finally, after her kids asked why she was always dropping everything; her wallet, the car keys, a pitcher of water, and the coffee pot, Maura visited her doctor.

After a battery of blood tests and review of her symptoms by an internal medicine physician, Maura received the shocking news that she suffered from lupus and fibromyalgia. Lupus is an autoimmune disease where the body attacks healthy tissue instead of only bacteria and viruses. Fibromyalgia is linked to overall pain, fatigue, and sleep disruption, among other things. The physicians told her that with her lean body she she was too fragile to take the risk of running or biking. They warned that if she fell, she would likely break bones.

The following summer in 2003, Maura had her diseases under control and her physician gave her the green light to begin exercising again. Maura said, "I reached the point where it seemed my diseases were taking control of my life. That's why I started with triathlon: to take back my life." After receiving an unelpful training guide from a group coach, she decided to train for her first Sprint triathlon, despite never having run before. Training wasn't always cut and dried, she says, "I had to train early in the morning because I'm highly allergic to the sun. I struggled, but worked through my symptoms with nutrition (she also had celiac disease—an allergy to gluten), medication, and ultimately alternative medicine (acupuncture)." Before the actual triathlon, Maura had only run two miles. She went on to race the short pool swim, six mile bike ride, and a 5K run—crossing the finish line feeling exhilarated and in control again. She wanted to do more.

Maura Kennedy

And she did. Maura's accomplishment that day led her to re-set new goals, and in 2004 she competed three more triathlons *and* ran her first half marathon (13.1 miles). She was on a high—accomplishing things her physicians thought she could never do. In 2005 she trained for Olympic distance triathlons and ran her second half marathon in March—the hilly Canamara, Ireland with her husband Ted.

Then, on a warm July morning in 2006, while cycling on a road a few miles from her home, Maura's life flashed before her eyes. It was 9:15 am, and she was riding west off the wooded bike trail onto the street toward a friend's house where she'd parked her car, when a young driver turned in front of her—not seeing Maura on her bike. She hit his car on the passenger's side and flew over his windshield, cracking it on the way. Her helmet splintered as she flipped over the car. She landed on her back. At the moment she collided with the car, a wave of selfishness flooded over her. "As I hit the car, I thought at least I was going to die doing what I love. When I hit the ground, I realized I was still alive—I could see my hand. I wondered if all my bones were broken." Then she began crying. The driver knelt down beside her and asked if she was seriously hurt. She said, "No, I'm just happy to hear your voice!"

Maura had neck strain, two herniated discs in her back, and bruises all over her body. She couldn't compete in the triathlon later that month, but her two oldest children did a kid's triathlon on her behalf. Maura was a proud mother. She took several months to recover and even the next year wasn't ready to mount a bike again. Her children nudged her to get back on her bike and train again— they told her she had to get back. With the support of her family, she shopped for a new bike and left the store with a new set of wheels.

Maura rode recreationally that year, taking her bike out Sunday mornings when traffic was light. Riddled with doubts about getting back into the tri scene, she faced another setback in 2008—a bout of mononucleosis from which she took months to recuperate, leaving her drained and unable to train.

It wasn't until 2010 when she met Libby at a mutual friend's house that she considered doing another triathlon. Inspired by Libby's enthusiasm, Maura joined the TWT women's group, planning to do "just a little bit." Since she was used to training by herself, instead of with a group, she was hesitant about the scheduled workouts. In the past, if she woke up stiff or tired, she's swap a run workout for a swim. It was easier not to have someone counting on her to show up. But after a few workout sessions, Maura realized training with a group helped push her to keep going and think positive thoughts.

Maura had a few flare ups that set her back, and she occasionally had to slow down or stop training for fear of getting too sick. The group helped her stay positive and look forward to workouts when she was ready. With the Trek Women's race around the corner, Maura's children urged her to enter the triathlon.

Despite having the stomach flu two weeks before the race, Maura slowly bounced back and had a couple of workouts the week before the race. During the race weekend, she stayed with her family at their cottage in Wisconsin. On Sunday morning, Maura's husband Ted awakened while it was still dark to drive her to Pleasant Prairie, Wisconsin where he planned to drop her at the entrance with her gear.

When they arrived, the road was blocked and they were directed to the shuttle area. Maura had to walk fast for 15 minutes to reach the transition area before it closed. As she was hustling and huffing, she realized she'd left her cycling helmet in the car. Breathing even heavier now, Maura called Ted, who was a step ahead—already on his bike bringing it to her. She met up with Ted, grabbed her helmet, and entered the transition area with five minutes to spare. She dropped her gear at a rack, using a red backpack at the end of her row as her marker. She speed-walked to the swim start, about a half mile from transition, snapped on her yellow swim cap, and saw a wave of women in yellow caps ready to leave and go in the water to start. "I forgot I had to go over the start pad to activate my chip and was ready to jump in from the edge of the lake. I talked to other women around me about the age group and realized I was in a different heat. I found my yellow capped age group, calmed down a bit, caught my breath, and asked a woman next to me about the course. She had done the Trek a few times and told me all about it before we started." Maura let out a deep sigh of relief.

After the swim, Maura saw Libby and Hope, who cheered her on. She wore a huge smile as she headed into T1. She kept saying her mantra over and over, "Nothing is going to happen to you. It's okay to push yourself."

On the course, Maura passed Ted and a friend's husband cheering, "Go Maura!" She saw Joni (Dobson), who'd gone off in an earlier wave, walking on the run path and they exchanged, "You go, girl!" as they passed one another.

Five years had passed since Maura crossed a finish line, and it felt incredible. She was back! She was again a triathlete, after all she'd been through. She accomplished her goal and stared down her fears.

Now Maura tells other women, "If you put your mind to it, you can accomplish anything, even if you have setbacks and disabilities. If you want to move on in life, you must face your fears. Fear can set you back and take a grip on your life. You can learn to face it and have the courage to move forward."

Looking back, Maura says, surviving the bike accident was a message that she wasn't meant to stop. Being a triathlete was her accomplishment, her identity.

Maura:

66 You don't know where life will take you, so you have to do things when you can. Doing triathlons is one of the best things I've ever done for myself. When you become a triathlete, you get to do something amazing. It belongs to you, and no one else. Being a triathlete gives you courage, strength, wisdom, and inspiration to carry through life. You're the one who sets the goals and you cross the finish line by yourself. This is one of the most rewarding journeys you'll ever take. 99

Elyse Tish: Discovering Where She Belongs

Elyse Tish researched dogs before finding the perfect dog for her family, then she took tap dancing lessons, learned how to do tanagrams (seven piece puzzles), and even chant. Since the age of 40, when Elyse read brain research suggesting we should always be learning, she set out to learn something new each year—either a mental or physical skill that required ongoing practice. Lifelong learning was a part of her yearly plan, so in 2009, when a work colleague wanted to improve her fitness, she suggested to Elyse they sign up for TWT and train for a triathlon together, so neither of them could chicken out.

Two weeks after the first group meeting, Elyse's friend's house burned, devastating her and her family. She dropped out of the program, but Elyse kept going, despite losing her support and not being athletic. Since high school she'd considered herself an intellectual and became a successful lawyer. She wasn't sure it was possible to also become an athlete.

Elyse Tish

Elyse had completed a 10K race the previous year, but ran a slow 12-minute mile pace. She ran with a friend who was a marathoner, and they finished together last in the field. When Elyse apologized to her friend for coming in last, she smiled and said, "You're still finishing ahead of all those people who are in bed!" Elyse brought this attitude to her tri training.

In the beginning, she couldn't swim the length of the pool without coming up gasping. And when it came to swimming in the lake, she was afraid she'd somehow get lost. When she attempted her first lake swim, clouds loomed in the sky, ready to burst with rain. Libby and Elyse stood on the beach looking out over the lake. They entered waist deep in their wetsuits and stood side by side, blowing bubbles in the water to get comfortable. Trembling, Elyse put her lips to the cool, murky, lake water and closed her eyes. Rain came drizzling down, but Libby urged Elyse to swim just five strokes out and five strokes back. She did. Then lightening flashed in the distance. The area warning bell sounded and they had to leave the water and head for shelter. Lesson over!

The next week they met again—same time, same lake—but this time Libby encouraged Elyse to swim to the 50 yard buoy and back.

Elyse swam stroke-by-stroke freestyle toward the buoy, stopping a few times to sight and get her bearings. She rounded the buoy and swam back to the beach—a first in her life.

When it came to cycling, Elyse was scared going 20 miles an hour, but she paced herself on the weekly rides. Her husband called her the most fear-bound athlete he'd ever known. Despite her apprehension, she continued to practice swimming, biking, and running with the TWT program and signed up for the Trek Women's Sprint distance tri in Wisconsin later that summer. Her goal was to finish the race in under two hours.

At her swim wave start, Elyse says, "I felt I was in over my head. I felt I didn't belong there." She shouted out to a "swim angel" (lifeguard) that she was panicking. The angel said, "Do you want a noodle?"

Elyse replied, "No, I just need to know you're watching me." Elyse calmed herself, took a deep breath, and kept swimming. She emerged from the lake feeling euphoric about her accomplishment.

At the end of the bike course, she saw her husband, her 14-year-old autistic son, and her sister who'd driven in to Pleasant Prairie to see her race. She ran the 5K at her usual pace, and her family found spots along the fence to cheer Elyse as she ran her final few yards to cross the finish line.

Elyse says, "I felt so good coming across the finish line, I knew I had to keep doing this!"

A few days after the race, the group gathered to celebrate their success. When each athlete had a moment to talk about her training and race experience, Elyse broke down in tears. She'd never considered herself an athlete and felt isolated from other women and parents because of having a special needs child. There, at the party, she belonged with the other athletes.

Elyse says, "It was an incredible feeling. I do belong in the lake and with this group of women. I belong to this club and the only real requirements are that you want to be there and you do the work.

It doesn't really matter if I run 12-minute miles, or that I wasn't a swimmer."

She gained confidence in all areas of her life by following the program, putting in the time, doing the workouts, and completing her goal. Now she's more concerned about her family's overall fitness and signs them up for 5K races. The next year she did the Trek, Glenview, and Danskin races and felt more at ease with each event. Elyse wasn't nervous, didn't panic in the water, and enjoyed every moment of each race.

Elyse:

66 When I started, I thought swimming a half-mile in open water would be impossible. But I did it, one stroke at a time. I believe in "big goals, small steps." That concept truly works with triathlon training. My success in finishing several Sprint triathlons convinced me that small steps could get my family to our big goal: independent living for my autistic son. By taking the time to train and giving myself something personal to do for myself, I gained confidence and camaraderie. I'm my own person, with my own friends; not just "Henry's mom." And my son and husband are proud of me, too. 99

Thank You
for Taking the Leap Into Triathlon

Have fun with your journey!
Tell us your story on www.trithejourney.com

NOTES

TRI NOTES
Journaling Pages

USE THIS JOURNAL TO WRITE ABOUT your thoughts, feelings, and day-to-day or week-to-week accomplishments or struggles. This is your space, for your eyes only. Journaling will help you track your progress and keep you moving forward.

We've included ideas to inspire your thinking and help you decide what to write in your TRI journal. These questions have worked for us, so were passing them on to you. Of course, feel free to write whatever comes to mind.

Journaling suggestions:

Training Start Date:

First day of training/workout session: what and where:

How I felt the first day of training:

What the weather was like:

What I was thinking while I worked out:

How I felt at the end of the workout:

What I ate and drank pre-workout and recovery:

Personal Goals:

~~~~JOURNAL PAGES~~~~

"Nothing great was ever achieved without enthusiasm."
-Ralph Waldo Emerson

Date: _____ Workout: _____

_____

_____

_____

_____

_____

_____

_____

_____

_____

_____

_____

_____

_____

_____

_____

_____

Positive Thought:

_____

_____

"If you do not hope, you will not find what is beyond your hopes."
-St. Clement of Alexandra

Date: _____ Workout: _____

_____

_____

_____

_____

_____

_____

_____

_____

_____

_____

_____

_____

_____

_____

_____

Positive Thought:

_____

_____

"There are some people who live in a dream world, and there are some who face reality. And then there are those who turn one into the other."
-Douglas Everett

Date: _____ Workout: _____

_____

_____

_____

_____

_____

_____

_____

_____

_____

_____

_____

_____

_____

_____

Positive Thought:

_____

_____

"Stop acting as if life is a rehearsal. Love this day as if it were your last. The past is over and gone, the future is not guaranteed."
-Wayne Dyer

Date: _____   Workout: _____

_____

_____

_____

_____

_____

_____

_____

_____

_____

_____

_____

_____

_____

_____

Positive Thought:

_____

_____

"You were born to win, but to be a winner, you must plan to win, prepare to win, and expect to win."
-Zig Zigler

Date: _____ Workout: _____

_____

_____

_____

_____

_____

_____

_____

_____

_____

_____

_____

_____

_____

_____

_____

Positive Thought:

_____

_____

"To try and fail is at least to learn,
To fail to try is to suffer the loss of what might have been."
-Ben Franklin

Date: _____ Workout: _____

_____

_____

_____

_____

_____

_____

_____

_____

_____

_____

_____

_____

_____

_____

_____

Positive Thought:

_____

_____

"Some people have thousands of reasons why they can not do what they want to, when all they need is one reason why they can."
~Willie Whitney

Date: _____ Workout: _____

_____

_____

_____

_____

_____

_____

_____

_____

_____

_____

_____

_____

_____

_____

_____

_____

Positive Thought:

_____

_____

"Yesterday is ashes, tomorrow is wood.
Only today does the fire burn brightly."
Old Eskimo saying

Date: _____ Workout: _____

_____

_____

_____

_____

_____

_____

_____

_____

_____

_____

_____

_____

_____

_____

_____

_____

Positive Thought:

_____

_____

"Every morning you are handed 24 golden hours. They are one of the few things in this world that you get free of charge. IF you had all the money in the world, you couldn't buy an extra hour. What will you do with this priceless treasure? Remember, you must use it, as it is given only once. Once wasted you can not get it back."

-Unknown

Date: _____   Workout: _____

_____

_____

_____

_____

_____

_____

_____

_____

_____

_____

_____

_____

_____

Positive Thought:

_____

_____

"When we are motivated by goals that have deep meaning, by dreams that need completion, by pure love that needs expressing, then we truly live life."
-Greg Anderson

Date: _____ Workout: _____

_____

_____

_____

_____

_____

_____

_____

_____

_____

_____

_____

_____

_____

_____

_____

_____

Positive Thought:

_____

_____

"There is no better time than right now to be happy,
Happiness is a journey, not a destination."
-Unknown

Date: _____ Workout: _____

_____

_____

_____

_____

_____

_____

_____

_____

_____

_____

_____

_____

_____

_____

_____

Positive Thought:

_____

_____

"Work like you don't need money, love like you've never been hurt,
and dance like no one's watching."
-Unknown

Date: _____ Workout: _____

_____

_____

_____

_____

_____

_____

_____

_____

_____

_____

_____

_____

_____

Positive Thought:

_____

_____

"The future belongs to those who believe in the beauty of their dreams."
-Eleanor Roosevelt

Date: _____ Workout: _____

_____

_____

_____

_____

_____

_____

_____

_____

_____

_____

_____

_____

_____

_____

_____

Positive Thought:

_____

_____

"When it comes to women and their bodies, God probably said:
Let there be flesh."
-Demetria Martinez, writer

Date: _____   Workout: _____

_____

_____

_____

_____

_____

_____

_____

_____

_____

_____

_____

_____

_____

_____

Positive Thought:

_____

_____

"Every great dream begins with a dreamer. Always remember, you have within you the strength, the patience, and the passion to reach for the stars to change the world."
-Harriet Tubman

Date: _____ Workout: _____

_____

_____

_____

_____

_____

_____

_____

_____

_____

_____

_____

_____

_____

_____

Positive Thought:

_____

_____

"Every day do something that will inch you closer to a better tomorrow."
-Doug Firebaugh

Date: _____ Workout: _____

_____

_____

_____

_____

_____

_____

_____

_____

_____

_____

_____

_____

_____

_____

_____

Positive Thought:

_____

_____

"What progress, you ask, have I made?
I have begun to be a friend to myself."
-Hecato, Greek philosopher

Date: _____ Workout: _____

_____

_____

_____

_____

_____

_____

_____

_____

_____

_____

_____

_____

_____

_____

_____

_____

Positive Thought:

_____

_____

"Change and growth take place when a person has risked himself and dares to become involved with experimenting with his own life."
-Herbert Otto

Date: _____ Workout: _____

_____

_____

_____

_____

_____

_____

_____

_____

_____

_____

_____

_____

_____

_____

_____

Positive Thought:

_____

_____

"If we all did the things we are capable of, we would astound ourselves."
-Thomas Edison

Date: _____ Workout: _____

_____

_____

_____

_____

_____

_____

_____

_____

_____

_____

_____

_____

_____

_____

_____

Positive Thought:

_____

_____

"Goals are the fuel in the furnace of achievement."
-Brian Tracy, *Eat that Frog*

Date: _____ Workout: _____

_____

_____

_____

_____

_____

_____

_____

_____

_____

_____

_____

_____

_____

_____

Positive Thought:

_____

_____

"Energy and persistence conquer all things."
-Benjamin Franklin

Date: _____ Workout: _____

_____

_____

_____

_____

_____

_____

_____

_____

_____

_____

_____

_____

_____

_____

_____

Positive Thought:

_____

_____

~~~~YOUR FINAL WORKOUT~~~~

Date: _____

Workout Details:

_____

_____

_____

_____

_____

_____

Positive Observations:

_____

_____

_____

_____

_____

Your Positive Affirmation:

_____

_____

_____

_____

RACE DAY:_____

APPENDIX

Off-Season Training

SINCE THE TYPICAL TRIATHLON RACE season occurs during the summer, when fall and winter arrive you'll find yourself with free time. Use these months to stay fit and maintain the endurance base you've established: plan your races (maybe a running race, or indoor sprint tri), then plan your workouts. For instance:

Mondays: 6 to 7 a.m. runs,

Wednesdays: 6 p.m. spin class,

Fridays: Fitness Pilates class,

Saturdays: family swim.

Make it work for your schedule, add variety, and make it enjoyable. Remain tri-focused a couple days a week, but add new things so you won't burn out before the regular season begins. To maintain your fitness level you should continue exercising a minimum of three days a week. To improve your level, work out in some way five days a week.

During this time, take the opportunity to work on your weakest sport, while including strength conditioning. Often off-season is when athletes focus on resting and rehabilitating a nagging injury and commit to a physical therapy regime. Don't go into your next season injured; come back stronger than ever and ready for the next challenge.

Suggestions for Off-Season Training:

- Masters swim team
- Weekly spin classes
- Weekly running group
- Pilates
- Yoga
- Boot camp
- Cross fit
- Weight training
- Zumba dance class

Strength circuits/swim workout
Warm up: Track 5 minutes

I. Circuits: 4 minutes each set: repeat exercises in succession for each circuit for the entire 4 minutes.

Circuit 1:
- 10 squats
- 10 dips
- 10 knee ups (run in place with high knees)

Circuit 2:
- 4 push up/side plank
- 10 jumping jacks
- 5 burpies (squat thrust) or 10 mountain climbs

Circuit 3:
- Lateral lunge alternate 10X total
- 10 pushups (arms close to sides working tri's)
- 10 forward lunges

Circuit 4:
- Calf raises 10 each side
- 20 jump rope
- 10 hamstring/glute press 5 each leg

In between circuit sets; Stairs/lunge circuit: X2
1. Run down and up steps X2.
2. Bunny hops or walking lunges, until stair cycle complete, switch

Back to set 2 of circuits:

II. **AB circuit:** 2 minutes each circuit
Set 1:
- In and extend X15
- Knees to elbow crunch X20

Continue Repeating

Set 2:
- Bicycle X20
- Plank 30 secs

Continue Repeating

Equipment:
Mats

Swim: Time trial
- 100 warm up (4 lengths)
- DRILL: Alternating Side balance 50 or right up left back
- 10 minute endurance swim. Record distance
- Drill: 50 Catch-ups
- 4X50's speed down, recovery back R 30
- Drill: 50 thumb thigh brush (practice full extension)
- Kick: 200
- Drill: 100 triple switch
- 4X100 70-80% time yourself, see if you can keep your pace or better for all 4
- 200 cool down

Favorite Triathlon Swim Drills

To become a more efficient swimmer, practice three main elements:

1. Balance
2. Extension/streamlining
3. Rotation

As you practice the following drills you'll find your technique improving and your effort decreasing, helping you become more efficient and confident. We suggest doing a few drills with each swim workout. Drills help instill proper technique. Even Olympic swimmers still do their drills, as should you.

Basic head-lead balance drill:

Goal: Basic balance, buoyancy, head position awareness

Do this:

Body in face down floating position, hands on thighs, eyes down, which will create a straight bodyline, and help raise your legs.

Kick easy flutter kick, breathing forward by lifting head up every 8-10 kicks; after each breath drop your head back down to the starting position (you should notice that when you lift your head your hips and legs sink) when your head position is back to neutral, your hips and legs rise again and your body is in a balanced position.)

Basic head-lead balance drill
Mary Bradbury

Forward balance with extended arms drill:

Goal: Continued balance, with arm extension, head position awareness and swimming 'taller' concept.

Do this:

Body in face down floating (or prone) position, arms extended reaching toward opposite side of the pool as feet are reaching, thumbs slightly touching to make a narrow "V." Head facing down, ears touching biceps.

Start the drill by pushing off wall in above position. After every 8-20 flutter kicks, raise your head for a breath, then lower your head and rebalance. You should notice that you are a little faster than with your arms to the side and that you are a longer, more streamlined swimmer. Remember Front Quadrant swimming concepts and elongation concepts in swim chapter.

Side balance drill:

Goal: Learn how to balance on both sides, continue practicing streamline low head position, and working on rotation, side breathing concepts.

Do this:

Bottom arm in the water extended straight over your head, and reaching toward the side of the pool you are swimming towards, top arm is extended towards other wall, relaxed resting on your top thigh.

Body is in side balance position, push off the wall, flutter kicking. Face is in the water (looking towards side wall or rotated in towards your arm pit), rotate your entire body to your back to take a breath then roll back to side balance position.

Top shoulder is visible above water.

Body is in a straight line from head to toe (remember the skewer concept, head position and body staying in a straight line and neutral, rotating around the skewer. Use a relaxed but steady kick. Practice on both sides.

Single-arm freestyle:

Goal: balance, rotation and elongation while pulling. Focus on maintaining body balance throughout the stroke as well as breathing while rotating. Putting the stroke together, focusing on one side at a time.

Single arm freestyle with high elbow
Mary Bradbury

Do this:

Flutter Kick 8-10 kicks while in forward balance head down (prone) position arms are extended toward the side of the pool you are swimming toward, head is tucked in between arms with ears near biceps, eyes facing down.

Pull with one arm and rotate the hips/body to the side as if doing side balance, with a pull added, bring the arm back to original stream line position, recover, and kick another 8-10 kicks prior to repeating, pull, rotation, breath, recover.

Practice on both sides, go down working on right side, back working on left.

Alternating side balance:

Goal: work on bilateral breathing as well as rotating form side to side incorporating all three cardinal rules, balance, extension, rotation.

Do this:

Start on your right side balance position. Left arm is extended in the water above your head, reaching for the end of the pool, the other arm extended and resting on your right thigh. Take a breath and transition by rotating your head toward the bottom of the pool as your top, right arm extends to meet the left, start a stroke and pull through the water with the left as you rotate to your left side balanced position. Repeat on each side, resting in side-balanced position for a breath before completing your stroke and rotation to the other side

Triple switch side balance:

Goal: Work on smoothly rotating from side to side, incorporating normal stroke, balance rotation, elongation and bilateral breathing,
Do this:

- Triple switch is similar to the Alternating Side Balance Drill but instead of taking one stroke to switch sides you take three.
- Start in side balanced position, take a breath, take three consecutive strokes, 1,2,3 and rotate to opposite side, take a breath, repeat 3 stokes, rotate, repeat.
- On the third stroke you should keep the lead arm extended and roll into the side balance position on the opposite side from where you started, top arm resting briefly on the top thigh.
- In the beginning glide for 5-8 seconds in the side balance position while you take a breath, once you have it mastered reduce the interval to 3 seconds, then a natural stroke breath time.

Full extension catch-up:

Goal: More closely approximates full stroke while maintaining balance, and extension, also focusing on that Front Quadrant swimming, keeping you swimming "tall."
Do this:

As you swim, wait to start your pull until the recovery arm enters the water and reaches full extension. You'll feel like your rhythm is off, but this actually helps you learn to take full advantage of your glide and to hold your streamline position and teach you not to start your pull too early. Remember the switch of the glove visual. The hand in the water is wearing a glove, the recovery hand enters the water and extends into the glove, just as you start your pull out of the glove, switching the glove.

Full extension, catch-up position before stroke is taken before starting next pull
Mary Bradbury

High elbow/fingertip drag:

Goal: works on the recovery of the stroke or the top arm. Helps keep elbows close and high for a more efficient recovery and entry. Helps combat "windmill arms."

Drag fingers across the top of the water, keeping a high elbow
Mary Bradbury

Do this:

- As your arm recovers, drag your thumb along the side of your body until it reaches your armpit.

- Drag your fingertips along the surface of the water until your hand enters.
- Keep your hand close to your head as you recover—your elbow should be higher than your hand.

Sighting freestyle:

Goal: Triathlon specific drill that reinforces good body position while navigating while in an open water swim.

Sighting freestyle
Kim Morgan

Do this:

- Swim freestyle and lift head out of the water to "sight" every 3-5 strokes.
- Maintain your normal body roll and a steady kick in order to keep proper body position.
- Work on recovering and rebalancing quickly in order to keep your efficiency.
- Once sighting becomes natural, you may find you only need to sight every 10 strokes. It depends on how straight you swim and how often you want to check your direction.

Swim Workouts		
Workout #1	SET	REST IN BETWEEN
Warm-up:	100 free	
Do twice:	1x50 catch-up	10 seconds
	1x50 streamline kicking	10 seconds
	3x100's build	15 seconds
	1x50 catch-up	20 seconds
	4x50's build	15 seconds
	1x50 catch-up	30 seconds
	4x25's build	10 seconds
	100 easy drill of your choice	
Total yardage:	1200	
Workout #2	SET	REST IN BETWEEN
Warm-up:	4x50's drill of your choice	10 sec
	100 kick	
	300 free- every 4th 25 is catch-up	20 sec
	200 free- every 3rd 25 is catch-up	20 sec
	100 free- the 1st & 4th 25's are catch-up	20 sec
	2x100 free- build	20 sec
	100 easy choice (backstroke, breaststroke, drill, etc)	
Total yardage:	1200	
Workout #3	SET	REST IN BETWEEN
Warm-up:	100 swim, 100 kick, 100 drill	15 sec
	8x75's (25 drill, 25 stroke count, 25 build)	20 sec
	300 (50 catch-up, 25 right arm, 25 left arm, 50 perfect)	
Total yardage:	1200	

Workout #4	SET	REST IN BETWEEN
Warm-up:	2x150 (50 drill, 50 kick, 50 swim)	15 sec
	4x50's build	15 sec
	1x100 fast	1 minute
	2x100 build	20 sec
	1x100 fast	1 min
	4x50's descend	15 sec
	2x50's fast	10 sec
	100 easy	
Total yardage:	1200	

Workout #5	SET	REST IN BETWEEN
Warm-up:	100 drill	
	4x25's DPS	15 sec
	100 negative split	15 sec
	4x25's Side Balance drill	15 sec
	150 (50 fist drill, 100 swim)	20 sec
	4x25's DPS	15 sec
	300 (sprint every 4th length)	20 sec
	4x25's Shark Fin 2	20 sec
	2x50's fast	20 sec
	100 easy	
Total yardage:	1250	

Workout #6	SET	REST IN BETWEEN
Warm-up:	100 side balance drill	
	100 single arm free (work on a high elbow on your pull)	
	300 think about nice long strokes	20 sec
	300 sprint every 4th 25	20 sec
	200 sprint every 4th 25	20 sec
	100 think about nice long strokes	20 sec
	2x25's sprint	10 sec
	50 double arm backstroke easy	
Total yardage:	1200	

AUTHOR BIOS

Elizabeth (Libby) Hurley is the founder and president of Together We Tri (TWT) a Chicago-area triathlon training program. Libby is a three-time Ironman finisher and veteran of more than 50 races.

Fueled by her background as a competitive age group swimmer with Olympic aspirations, Libby longed to compete in triathlons. Lack of information on the emerging sport led Libby to devise a training program for herself—a program she would later use to inspire her entrepreneurial quest.

Tri the Journey is the culmination of Libby's desire to help people everywhere experience the joy of triathlons. The book and website are the realization of Libby's dream to encourage thousands more to experience a fitness program that will transform lives.

Since 2000, Together We Tri and has trained and motivated more than 6,000 athletes to reach their triathlon goals.

Prior to founding Together We Tri, Libby worked as a physician's assistant, specializing in neurosurgery and neuroresearch. She is a graduate of the University of Kentucky and currently resides in Glenview, Illinois with her husband and three children.

Elizabeth (Betsy) Noxon is a freelance health and fitness writer whose work has appeared in numerous national magazines, including *AARP The Magazine*, *Better Homes & Gardens*, *Experience Life*, *Health*, *Heart-Healthy Living*, *Parents*, *Runner's World*, and United Airline's *Hemispheres*. She has also reported on health conferences for Glamour magazine, written online for MSN.com Health & Fitness, Livestrong. com, for *The Chicago Tribune*, *The L.A. Times*, *North Shore* magazine and for corporate clients.

An athlete all her life, Betsy is always on the go, be it running, swimming, cycling, skiing or golfing. A cycling trip down California's Highway One inspired her to take up triathlons. Training with Together We Tri since 2008, Betsy has competed in eight triathlons, including the 2010 USA Triathlon National Age Group Championships (a qualifying event). She was also named an Illinois State Champion in 2010.

Prior to her freelance writing career, Betsy worked in health care for a cardiovascular prevention program and as a practice manager for a large hospital system in Cleveland, Ohio.

Betsy is a member of the American Society of Journalists and Authors, Inc. She continues to her personal training, is a coach for Girls on the Run, and plans to continue competing as a triathlete. She resides in Glenview, Illinois with her husband and two children.

INDEX

Available from NorlightsPress and
fine booksellers everywhere

Toll free: 888-558-4354   **Online:** www.norlightspress.com

Shipping Info: Add $2.95 for first item and $1.00 for each additional item

Name_____

Address_____

Daytime Phone_____

E-mail_____

No. Copies	Title	Price (each)	Total Cost

		Subtotal	
		Shipping	
		Total	

Payment by (circle one):

   Check   Visa   Mastercard   Discover   Am Express

Card number_____3 digit code_____

Exp.date_____ Signature_____

Mailing Address:

2323 S.R. 252
Martinsville, IN 46151

Sign up to receive our catalogue at
www.norlightspress.com

LaVergne, TN USA
17 January 2011
212789LV00004B/1/P

9 781935 254355